George & Margaret Menzies
158 Claremont, Alloa
Clackmannanshire
FK10 2ER
01259 213213
g.menzies@btinternet.com

*THE ISLANDS SERIES*

# SIX INNER HEBRIDES

The author of *Six Inner Hebrides* has known the islands and their people intimately for many years. He has studied their history and in this concise, comprehensive account he provides with infectious enthusiasm the information the visitor wants. His book will make a visit wellnigh irresistible and it will be enjoyed nostalgically by those who already know these much loved islands.

# THE ISLANDS SERIES

\* Published in the United States by Stackpole
All other titles published in the United States by David & Charles Inc
The series is distributed in Australia by Wren Publishing Pty Ltd, Melbourne

_Wallace Menzies_

# SIX INNER HEBRIDES

Eigg Rum Canna Muck Coll Tiree

*by NOEL BANKS*

## DAVID & CHARLES

NEWTON ABBOT LONDON NORTH POMFRET (VT) VANCOUVER

In memory of
DONALD MACDONALD KIRK
of Laig Farm, Eigg
born on 25 April 1932
died on 1 May 1975

'. . . as complete an islander as the mind can figure'

—*Samuel Johnson*

ISBN 0 7153 7368 4

Library of Congress Catalog Card Number:
76-58786

Set in 11 on 13pt Linotype Baskerville and printed in
Great Britain by Latimer Trend & Company Ltd Plymouth
for David & Charles (Publishers) Limited
Brunel House   Newton Abbot   Devon

Published in the United States of America
by David & Charles Inc
North Pomfret   Vermont 05053   USA

Published in Canada
by Douglas David & Charles Limited
1875 Welch Street   North Vancouver   BC

# CONTENTS

*All uncredited photographs are by the author*

# *1*   SETTING

BEYOND the lonely lighthouse on Ardnamurchan Point, the westernmost tip of the British mainland, six islands lie scattered on the Sea of the Hebrides. Twelve miles to the east of north, a crenellated ridge on Eigg ends abruptly in the hooked and overhung Sgurr. Past the low hump of Muck, the Rum Coolins rake the northern sky, framed by the double wedge of Canna and the distant needles of the Skye Coolins. Close in to westward a tight group of islets and a sandy shore mark the end of Coll, which stretches south-west in a line of barren hillocks. Thirty miles away, beyond Coll, the little hills of Tiree may just be seen. Edged with surf, alive with the vivid colours that go with a clean atmosphere, this is Scotland's finest seascape.

On plan the six islands form an L-shaped archipelago: from an apex at the north of Eigg the shorter limb runs 20 miles north-west across Rum to Canna, the longer 40 miles south-west across Muck and Coll to Tiree. Although grouped with the Inner Hebrides, all six islands are oceanic. Seen from London perhaps the most significant thing about their position is not its 400 miles north but its 250 west; Eigg is westward of Land's End. Tiree is beyond the Isles of Scilly.

These islands, much closer to the Faroes than to London, lie on the very edge of Europe. They have a frontier quality at once their greatest handicap and their greatest attraction. It raises costs and limits amenity; but it also makes neighbourly help a prime virtue, breeds jacks-of-all-trades who cannot afford to be masters of none, and helps bind together small communities liable to internal stresses unknown in

7

larger human settlements. Small these communities certainly are. In 1971 Eigg, Rum, Canna and Muck, appropriately known as Small Isles, had 166 people on their 72 square miles; Coll had 145 on 28 sq miles and Tiree 865 on 30 sq miles. The total population was 1,176. The graphs on pages 68–70, 105, 110, 111, show that it has long been falling: it was 3,079 in 1901 and 7,065 in 1821. The islands' principal business has long been the breeding of beef cattle and sheep (or calves and lambs), generally for finishing elsewhere. Tiree is let to crofter tenants; good soils, a relatively dry climate and hard work have made this flattest of all the Hebrides into Scotland's most successful crofting area. Rum is a mountain laboratory for the Nature Conservancy, exporting venison and esoteric scientific papers; all its people are incomers since the Conservancy took over in 1957. The native islanders are basically bilingual Gaelic Scots, although Gaelic speech is diminishing. Island faiths are diverse. Eigg and Canna's Roman Catholicism may stem directly from St Columba. There are Church of Scotland congregations on all islands except Canna, the Free Church is represented on Coll and the Baptists on Tiree; Sabbatarianism is now in decline.

All the islands have great beauty. Seen from Eigg harbour the gnarled Sgurr rears 1,200ft above wooded slopes seemingly soft as the hills of Surrey, to face a stupendous panorama of mainland mountains. A summer day can be passed on Laig Bay, the west shore of Eigg, watching cloud-patterns flow over the chameleon cones of the Rum Coolins, across a sea punctured by plummeting gannets. The 2-mile curve of Coll's Crossapol Beach develops with such mathematical precision that the heart aches at its infinite beauty, and for its emptiness. White Tiree cottages, some demurely thatched and pretty as a pantomime-set, some grimly tarred and felted, crouch on a flower-strewn machair under the great dome of a maritime sky. Each island has some barren moor, but even that has its own attractions of waving cotton-grass and lochans that can gleam like jewels. Few places are more than 2 miles from the sea—one is always conscious of insularity. Any high

8

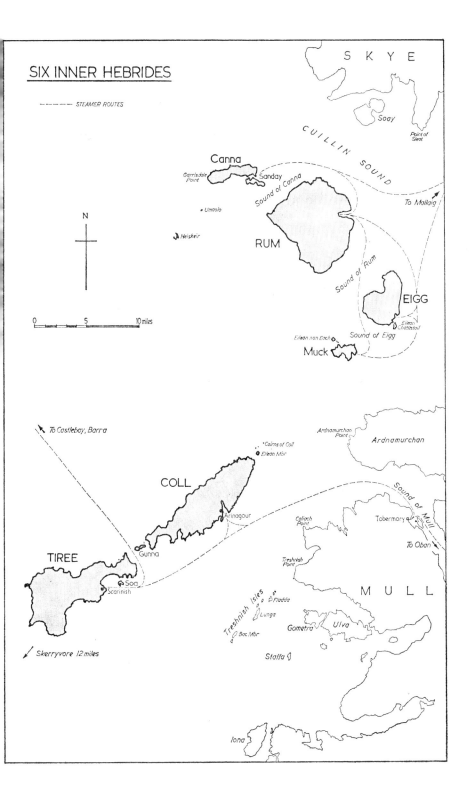

SIX INNER HEBRIDES

--- STEAMER ROUTES

S K Y E

Soay

Point of Sleat

CUILLIN SOUND

Canna

Garrisdale Point

Sanday

Sound of Canna

To Mallaig

Umaola

Heiskeir

RUM

Sound of Rum

EIGG

Eilean Chatastoil

N

0    5    10 miles

Eilean nan Each

Sound of Eigg

Muck

To Castlebay, Barra

Cairns of Coll

Eilean Mòr

Ardnamurchan Point

Ardnamurchan

COLL

Sound of Mull

Arinagour

Caliach Point

Tobermory

Gunna

Treshnish Point

To Oban

TIREE

Soa

Scarinish

M U L L

Treshnish Isles

Fladda

Lunga

Gometra

Ulva

Bac Mòr

Skerryvore 12 miles

Staffa

Iona

ground will reveal views of breathtaking beauty across to the other islands of the group.

Yet can these six islands fairly be called a group? Small Isles are an entity. Coll and Tiree form a single parish and were long linked by ferry across Gunna Sound. In the nineteenth century many Coll and Tiree folk were employed on Small Isles, and vice-versa, and several Small Isles' parish ministers were Collachs. Once the islands were served by a common steamer service. Now it is difficult to find anyone on Small Isles who has ever been to Coll or Tiree, which is hardly surprising—by public transport the journey takes twenty-four hours. Perhaps that does not matter overmuch; but isolation from central Scotland does. Tiree has a year-round air service to Glasgow, but most people go by boat to the Oban railhead; Tiree to Glasgow takes $9\frac{1}{2}$ hours for a straight-line distance of 107 miles. Small Isles' boat runs to the railhead at Mallaig. Canna to Glasgow, 117 miles direct, may be accomplished twice a week in 12 hours. Small Isles' facilities for sending off cattle and sheep (their vital exports) by public transport would be laughable if they were not potentially tragic: two boats a *year*, and no certainty that even those will be provided.

Such isolation gives the visitor a satisfying feeling of 'getting away from it all'. The Londoner may reflect as he steps gingerly from the steamer on to the Eigg ferry (Eigg, Rum and Muck have no steamer pier) that an airliner could have taken him across the world in the seventeen hours since he joined the sleeper at Euston. It could not have taken him anywhere lovelier, or quieter—once the small bustle of the ferry's arrival has died away and Eigg pier is again deserted. All is colour—purple hill, orange tangle, cream shore, black skerries where grey seals sleep in the sunshine, rainbow surf, green pellucid sea. Light itself seems coloured. There is a touch of the tropics about the sheltered head of the harbour as it dreams away the summer afternoon, its silence broken by a curlew's call, its stillness by the slow flap of a heron trailing his legs from sandbank to shore.

Johnson and Boswell wrote accounts of Coll during their involuntary visit in 1773. The only other widely known reference to any of the islands occurs in Robert Louis Stevenson's words to the *Skye Boat Song*:

> Mull was a-stern
> Rum on the port
> Eigg on the starboard bow . . .

Romantic enough. But the islands' history is largely tragic. They saw massacre in clan times, exploitation when their chiefs became absentee rent-collectors, and wholesale emigration in the bitter years of the nineteenth century. Yet because the people were Gaelic there was laughter as well as hardship in the dark cabins of the island clachans, and song and story amid the thick peat smoke.

Most islanders have prospered since World War II, and now many are within sight of owning the soil they cultivate, a thing their ancestors scarcely dreamed of. But the youngsters still leave, and the future lies shrouded in the soft sea mists.

# 2           SCENE

## GENERAL GEOLOGY

GNARLED and hummocky Lewisian gneiss, perhaps 1,000 million years old, predominates on Coll and Tiree. It probably lies under Small Isles, beneath Torridonian strata which surface to form northern Rum. Above the Torridonian the Great Estuarine series outcrops sporadically on Eigg and Muck. Those ancient sedimentary rocks apart, almost all Eigg, Canna and Muck are formed from residual fragments of vast sheets of igneous lava which, 40 million years ago, covered the whole Hebridean area. The Rum Coolins are denuded fragments of one of the local volcanoes. During this Tertiary period there was much land movement: a fault between Eigg and Rum may be one cause of their marked geological differences.

In glacial times Coll and Tiree may still have been mere hummocks on an extensive plateau, but Eigg, Rum, Canna and Muck were already separate islands. Ice from Mull and the mainland swept up surface soils and left only scanty deposits of boulder clay. During and after glaciation the land sank, then rose in stages, forming raised beaches.

## EIGG

Eigg (pronounced Egg), a kidney-shaped island measuring 5 miles by 3, is 7 miles from Rhu Point Arisaig and 15 from Mallaig, the port and railhead. Its sixty-nine people live at Galmisdale and Kildonnan in the south-east, and at Cuagach and Cleadale behind Laig Bay in the north-west. These sparse settlements are connected by a road traversing a faulted depression between the northerly 1,000ft (304m) plateau of Beinne Bhuidhe and a wet southern moorland dominated by a mile-long ridge of naked rock terminating in An Sgurr, the most memorable landmark in Hebridean seas. The central depression, said to look like a notch, may have given the island its name—*Eilean Eige*, Island of the Notch. *Egea* appears in Adamnan's seventh-century *Life of St Columba*. Spelling has varied: *Eig* was current in the nineteenth century.

Coasts are ironbound or scree except at each end of the central depression. There are shell-sand beaches around Galmisdale harbour. The mailboat does not venture into that rock-beset haven; the ferry meets her off Castle Island. Plantations of conifers and beautiful mixed woodland, put down during the century following 1840, soften the island scene, adorn the Lodge grounds and diversify birdlife, but many trees are now in decay.

The northern plateau and the southern moorland are structurally of basalt. As each basalt flow cooled, vertical contraction-joints tended to form closely packed hexagonal columns, as on Castle Island. Thick columns formed at lower levels, which cooled slowly. Thinner specimens occurred at mid-depth and were particularly liable to bending by later ground movement, as along the eastern cliffs. The top of a flow, which cooled quickly, formed a slag honeycombed by gas-voids (amygdaloids) which later filled with other minerals, occasionally of beautiful crystalline form—as around Rubh an Tangaird, the southern point (where there is also a striking perched needle). One need not go beyond the main road verge to see how the upper slag-basalt layer has crumbled to a rich chocolate soil. That ideal mixture, basalt soil and shell-sand (which adds lime and improves drainage), may be seen in the fields around the harbour and at Kildonnan. Kildonnan beach sand contains 30 per cent calcium carbonate and has been approved for fertiliser grant.

Sedimentary rocks underlie the basalt. Perhaps the oldest

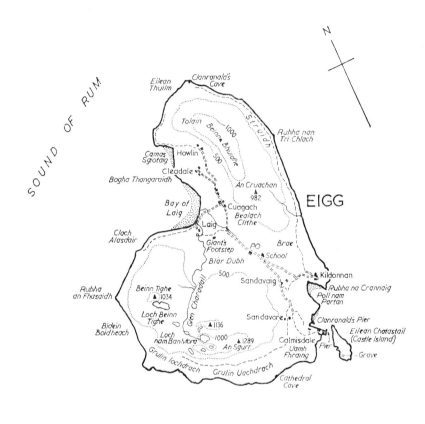

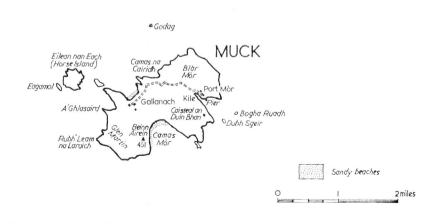

SOUND OF RUM

Eilean Thuilm
Clanranald's Cave
Rubha nan Tri Chlach
Tolain
Beinn Bhuidhe
Siffuidh
1000
500
Camas Sgrotaig
Howlin
Cleadale
Bogha Thangaraidh
An Cruachan
982
EIGG
Bay of Laig
Cuagach
Bealach Clithe
Laig
Clach Alasdair
Giant's Footstep
Brae
PO
School
Blar Dubh
Kildonnan
Beinn Tighe
1034
500
Sandavaig
Rubha na Crannaig
Poll nam Partan
Rubha an Fhasaidh
Loch Beinn Tighe
Glen Charadail
1136
Sandavore
Clanranald's Pier
Bidein Boidheach
Loch nam Ban Mora
1000
An Sgurr
1289
Calmisdale
Uamh Fhraing
Eilean Chatastail (Castle Island)
Pier
Grave
Grulin Iochdrach
Grulin Uachdrach
Cathedral Cave

SOUND OF EIGG

Godag

Eilean nan Each (Horse Island)
Camas na Cairidh
Blàr Mòr
MUCK
Eagamol
Port Mòr
A'Ghlasaird
Gallanach
Kile
Pier
Caisteal an Duin Bhan
Bogha Ruadh
Dubh Sgeir
Rubh'Leam na Laraich
Glen Martin
Beinn Airein
451
Camas Mòr

Sandy beaches

0        1        2 miles

are the Lower Estuarine shales, seen around sea level at Kildonnan. Intersected by intrusive basalt sills, they rise along the eastern cliffs and round the north point, sinking again to the shore at Camas Sgiotaig. These shales are rich in fossils. In loose red blocks on the north-point foreshore that lively geologist Hugh Miller, who visited the island in 1845–6, went 'hunting dead crocodiles' and found plesiosaurian vertebrae and ribs.

Above the shales are thick beds of Great Estuarine sandstone which appear in the eastern cliffs, round the north point, and continue southwards. Behind Camas Sgiotaig they have weathered into arches, doorways, windows, overhanging canopies and a gigantic mushroom. Miller wrote the first account of Camas Sgiotaig's singing sand ('sounding sand' in the last century):

> I struck it obliquely with my foot, where the surface lay dry . . . and . . . elicited a shrill sonorous note . . . I walked over it, striking it obliquely with each step, and with every blow the shrill note was repeated. My companions joined me: and we performed a concert in which, if we could boast of but little variety in the tones produced, might at least challenge all Europe for an instrument of the kind which produced them.

The sound has been described in various fanciful ways—'like an Aeolian harp'. A similar noise may be made by walking in coarse corduroy trousers. Appendix A contains notes on this odd phenomenon—only heard when the sand is dry.

Sandstone and limestone form unstable seacliffs between Camas Sgiotaig and Laig Bay. Immense blocks have moved away from the main face, leaving narrow passageways, hanging gardens where Grass of Parnassus flourishes, and secret waterfalls. At Bogha Thangaraidh lime pockets in the sandstone have recrystallised into concretionary nodules, occasionally 10ft (3m) in diameter. Down on the tidal rock-ledge, leaching of sandstone from around smaller nodules has left them imprisoned in rocky cages, in which they move about with a lugubrious rattling as the tide advances. Erosion has made this ledge a natural rock-garden, with miniature underground galleries, salty streams and limpid pools where sea-anemones bend and waver. Green beards of seaweed and tiny shells, pink and green and mottled orange, take the place of flowers.

Behind the dunes that fringe the lime-rich sands of Laig Bay the quiet fields of Cleadale lie on boulder clay left by glaciation from the 'notch'. The glacier gouged out a shallow tidal 'harbour' between Cleadale and Laig which lasted into the nineteenth century. The prow and sternpost of an uncompleted Viking-type ship were dug out hereabouts in the 1870s, and a rock below Bealach Clithe, a third of a mile from the shore, is still called *Sron Laimrhig*, Headland of the Landing-place.

Inland cliffs, the edge of the Beinn Bhuidhe plateau, ring the fertile Cleadale basin and culminate in a pulpit-rock reared against the sky—*Bidein an Tighearna*, the Pinnacle of the Lord. These 1,000ft cliffs too are unstable, for the basalt plateau, founded on the easily eroded Great Estuarine series, is fraying round its edges. The talus slopes are blanketed by birch scrub and burrowed by Manx shearwaters; gigantic debris extends below them for half a mile. The streams that drop over the cliff-edge gurgle beneath this chaotic country to emerge in springs like *Tobar Challuim Chille*, St Columba's Well, at the Cleadale roadside. The Giant's Footstep lochan above Laig Farm was formed between the forward edge of slipped material and the residual cliff, its orientation confirming a tradition that the giant was on his way to Rum. Of late the cliffs have been free from giants, but slipping continues. In 1950 a Cuagach croft-house was wrecked by a superficial slide following several days of continuous rain, and now lies smothered beneath the fuchsia and honeysuckle of its abandoned garden. Swinburne would have loved it.

The Sgurr ridge, a mile of mural black rock, is the largest mass of columnar pitchstone in the British Isles. It runs from the sea cliffs of Bidein Boidheach and Beinn Tighe in the

1 Across the water: *(above)* Poll nam Partan from the lonely road near Kildonnan, Eigg. Castle Island is across the water and Moidart, the country of Prince Charles Edward, in the background *(John Currie)*;
2 *(below)* the 'Kingdom whose summits are lower than the waves'. Sunset over Tiree *(Adam Collection)*

3 Peaks: *(above)* An Sgurr of Eigg, 1,289 ft *(John Currie)*;
4 *(below)* a thousand feet up in the wet desert of central Rum, Hallival and
Askival from Loch Gainmhich *(Dr W. A. Clark)*

west to the 1,289ft (390m) An Sgurr itself, sheer on two faces and overhanging at the front. The pitchstone is merely perched on a basalt surface sloping steeply from north to south, coated with a layer of agglomerate. Erosion at the pitchstone/basalt junction has formed a gallery 10ft high and 20ft wide on the southern face, roofed by the ends of pitchstone columns and floored by agglomerate containing Torridonian sandstone and fossil pine-wood. Rival theories on the origin of the Sgurr ridge were advanced by Sir Archibald Geikie, Director of the Geological Survey, and Professor Alfred Harker, author of the 1908 Geological Memoir. In Geikie's view successive layers of pitchstone flowed sub-aerially into a river valley eroded in the basalt, and the ridge-shape was exposed when the flanking basalt denuded away. The river originated in the Torridonian country of Wester Ross. He did not explain why such a short length of his valley became filled; although 'downstream' Heiskeir Island is wholly pitchstone, 'upstream' in Wester Ross no evidence of pitchstone remains. Harker thought the ridge was the remains of a pitchstone sill intruding the basalt, a theory that accounts more readily for two pitchstone dykes at Rubh an Tangaird (on the south coast of the island) which look like contorted coal-seams. The ridge is best viewed from the old track from Galmisdale to the Grulins, above the southern shore. Steep debris-slopes lead up to the face where myriads of columns are clearly seen —some upright, some inclined like multiple buttresses.

The pitchstone ridge provides a magnificent hill walk. One is torn between the majesty of the view and the interest and difficulty of walking over the rounded ends of columns; the surface is like a cobbled street contorted by an earthquake. The utterly deserted land to the north carries several lochs. On a sunny day they glint and gleam against their black rock setting but, when the high tops are lost in a moving mist, brooding mystery haunts this wilderness, and echoes from An Sgurr may chill the lonely walker. The Eigg folk peopled these lochs with half-human beings, kelpies and water-horses, and told tales of a Viking fort on the islet in Loch nam Ban

Mora, still approached by a sunken causeway of columnar rock.

On the south coast, at Upper Grulin, house-sized pitchstone blocks broken from the ridge and carried by a short glacier lie haphazard on a sweet greensward. Among them are the pathetic remains of tiny stone cabins made from columnar fragments, abandoned over a century ago.

### RUM

Rum is the largest, wettest, most barren and most deserted of the six islands. It is arguably the most mountainous island in Britain. Sgurr nan Gillean rises from sea level to 2,503ft (759m) in $\frac{3}{4}$ mile. These brittle peaks and rounded domes are like mountains drawn by a child—deficient in the horizontal.

No one knows how the island got its name. 'Spacious', 'extensive' and 'ridged' are translations from possible Gaelic roots, and 'roaring' from the Norse. It was spelt Rum and pronounced Roo-im by the indigenous population, long scattered over the face of the globe. Incomers preferred to rhyme it with 'Mum' and, for some reason never satisfactorily explained, to spell it Rhum—as it appears on an 1843 gravestone commemorating the wife of the island's manager, certainly not a native. The Ordnance Surveyor's Name Book shows Rum, but current published maps use Rhum. The Nature Conservancy decided to keep the 'h' because (according to their Gaelic authority) Rum ought to be spelt with an inconvenient accent over the 'u'.

The island is shaped like a diamond in a pack of playing-cards. Each axis measures about 8 miles. Four valleys radiate from a relatively low-lying centre. One runs north to the sands of Kilmory; another east to Kinloch at the head of the mile-long Loch Scresort, the only inlet and anchorage; a third south-west to Harris Bay, and a fourth west to Guirdil. Rough tracks connect Kinloch, Kilmory and Harris. Once there were villages at the seaward end of each valley; now the whole population of forty lives at Kinloch, in houses dominated

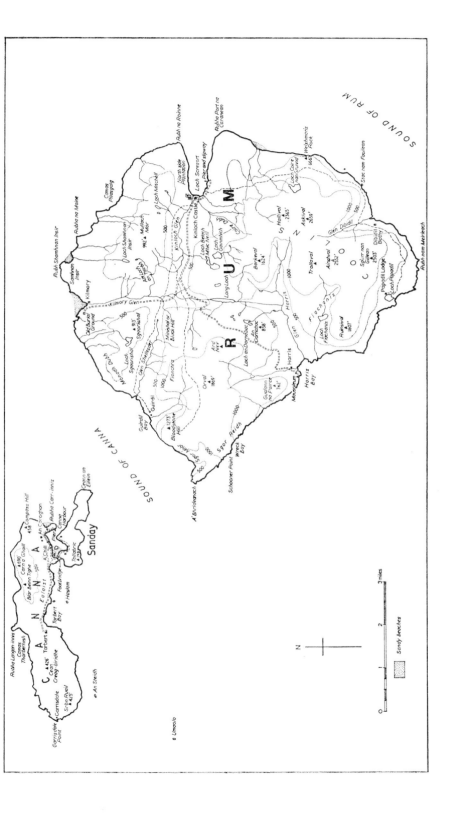

by a grand 'castle' built from Arran sandstone in the high noon of Edwardian extravagance.

Rum rests on Lewisian gneiss. Torridonian grit is exposed throughout the north of the island, rising to 992ft (301m) on Mullach Mor; this land is clothed with heather and mottled dull red by outcropping terraces. There is clearer colour in the sparse links and dunes of Kilmory and Samhnan Insir; round to the west the long, green, shoreward slopes at Guirdil contrast with the massive screes that buttress Bloodstone Hill off the shore. This is the end of the Torridon country. Bloodstone's fine crown is sculptured from the igneous lava mugearite, some of which contains 25 per cent of amygdales filled with agate, heliotrope, jasper, opal, zeolite and the eponymous bloodstone—a source for Neolithic toolmakers, and of jewellery and furniture inlays during the last century. Torridonian shales extend southwards from Loch Scresort past the sea-precipice at Welshman's Rock and the splendid canyon of the Dibidil River to Papadil, the southernmost point of the island. This country looks bare indeed. Its thin soils, leached by heavy rainfall, are washed away down the long steep slopes; the landscape is empty, without trees or bushes, or even a patterning of stone walls. But beyond stand the cones and spires of the Coolins.

What grand names the Vikings gave them: Barkeval, Hallival, Askival, Trollaval, Ainshval, Ruinsival! Only Sgurr nan Gillean is Gaelic—perhaps deriving from the Maclean (Mac-Gillean) clan who peopled Rum for half a millennium. For all their grandeur the Coolins are mere weathered serrations on the surface of a volcanic root 40,000ft (12,000m) deep. Ainshval and Sgurr nan Gillean are made of felsite. They are surrounded from north-east to south-west by an arc of ultra-basic strata, which builds the other main peaks; granophyre extends westwards to a line of stupendous inland cliffs, reaching 1,869ft (556m) on Orval. At Bloodstone the Torridonian is again encountered. The Coolins formed plutonically beneath earlier basalt, straining it and so accelerating denudation. The only basalt fragments remaining are

Minishal and Fionchra, shapely hills which close the view up Loch Scresort; their soils are the best on the island.

Glaciation was generally westwards but striations show that the Coolins induced a northward component. Mica-schist erratics from the mainland are present to about 1,750ft (530m). Morainic drift occurs in the lee of Askival and Hallival and on Dibidil valley floor. A useful boulder clay was deposited around Harris, Guirdil and Kinloch. Because the coasts are steep-to there was little room for raised beaches. The 100ft (30m) storm beach at Harris is more picturesque than useful, but the small beaches at Guirdil and Kilmory add a little to the island's limited area of cultivable ground, as did a 40ft (12m) beach at Kinloch, known as the Great Meadow until the Castle policies were laid out there. River alluvium occurs in Kilmory valley and around Kinloch and Glen Shellesder; at Kilmory it is enriched by blown sand. The deep peat beds which extend up Kinloch valley were used by Canna and Muck folk after their own mosses were stripped, and by the Castle in Edwardian times.

Rum was once extensively wooded. Deforesting increased erosion. Over-population led to over-intensive use of what useful soils there were. Under-capitalisation meant that little new ground was got by drainage. Overstock caused deterioration of upland pastures, and after the people were cleared in 1826 their patches of arable were surrendered to sheep. Finally the whole island became a man-made desert, its only oasis at Kinloch, its only crop venison. The ecological history of Rum is that of vast areas of the Highlands.

CANNA

Canna, 24 miles from Mallaig and 22 from South Uist, is out in the ocean. Extending 5 miles from east to west but only 1 mile from north to south, it is the only Hebridean island so orientated. The eastern half reaches 690ft (209m) and the western 426ft (129m); both are grassy basalt plateaux terraced south, with bird-haunted seacliffs on the north. The tidal satellite Sanday (formerly Sand Island) is connected by a ford and public footbridge. Ten crofts occupy its eastern end. The western end and all Canna are farmed by the proprietor. The thirty-three inhabitants live on Sanday and around the harbour, a sheltered stretch of water between the two islands. There is a steamer pier built and extended by successive proprietors, who also planted some lovely woodland.

Gaelic *Cana* means 'porpoise', a common mammal around the coasts in summer; or the name may be from *Kanin,* Isle of Rabbits. The eighteenth-century version was Cannay, which has a ring about it.

Canna and Sanday exhibit the regular terracing and plateau-type scenery resulting from successive basalt flows. Fragments of Torridonian are found in the agglomerates and water-sorted conglomerates which are particularly well developed at the east end, and on Sanday. They are (or were) locally called 'plumb-pudding' rock; the 'plumbs' are basalt blocks, sandstones and schists, probably broken down by volcanic movement. According to Geikie the conglomerates were laid down by a river flowing from the direction of the mainland across a basalt plain. Compass Hill contains enough permanently magnetised basalt to affect a compass reading. Aberrations at the surface of this 458ft (139m) cliff vary from 18° west to 60° east.

Glacial erratics are common around sea level. Granite boulders and red Torridonian material probably came from Rum, quartzites from the mainland. The ice left boulder clay in the easterly valley of Sanday; similar material was re-formed into the 70ft (23m) beach at Tarbert and the 100ft (32m) beach between Coroghan and Canna House. Peat is sparse, perhaps because of the good drainage inherent in the steep slopes and simple shapes of both islands. The well-drained basalt-bound conglomerates around the harbour and on Sanday produce excellent soils in conjunction with blown sand. There is good shelter from all directions except east. Spring sunshine hours are high. These favourable factors lead to spectacular results. 'Anything will grow here that can be protected . . . fuchsia, veronica, globe artichokes and all kinds of soft and hard fruit.' Daffodils are out in January.

## Heiskeir of Canna

Three miles south-west of Canna, the basalt rock Umaolo rises 24ft from the sea; 4 miles farther out lies Heiskeir, a mass of pitchstone columns $\frac{3}{4}$ mile from east to west and $\frac{1}{2}$ mile from north to south, carrying many glacial erratics. A sound of limpid water 200yd wide separates the western rock Garbh Sgeir from the eastern 'mainland', maximum height 34ft above sea level. At low tide the 'mainland' is traversed by narrow inlets, one of which broadens into a steep-sided lagoon where boats may shelter from Atlantic storms whilst spume drives overhead. At high tide, channels separate the 'mainland' into three or more parts.

Until the 1890s, and perhaps afterwards, Canna cattle grazed Heiskeir's 10 acres of sparse but succulent summer grasses and drank its fresh spring water. Now three light-house-keepers share the island with Atlantic seals, crabs and lobsters innumerable, kittiwakes, common and Arctic terns, eider ducks and (unless a grass fire in the 1960s wiped them out) green-veined, white and common blue butterflies; bumblebees drone around yellow flag iris on the old summer-sheiling land. Bridges have been thrown over the inlets and, behind high walls built against the ocean gales, the keepers grow flowers and vegetables in the most remote of island gardens.

### MUCK

This relatively low-lying island of $2\frac{1}{2}$ sq miles is isolated even in Hebridean terms, although only 8 miles from Ardnamurchan. Not until 1966 was it first served regularly by public transport. Muck is totally exposed from south-east round to north-west. The map shows an indented coastline with much sheltered water but geology inhibits its use. This is basalt country with typical horizontal terracing; perhaps because slopes are gentler and coasts less steep than on Eigg

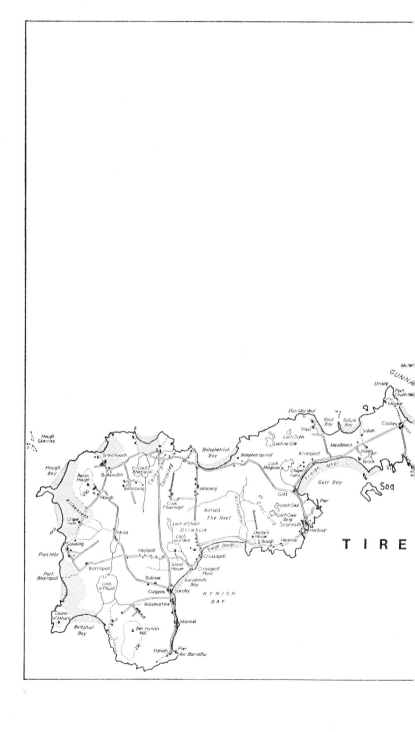

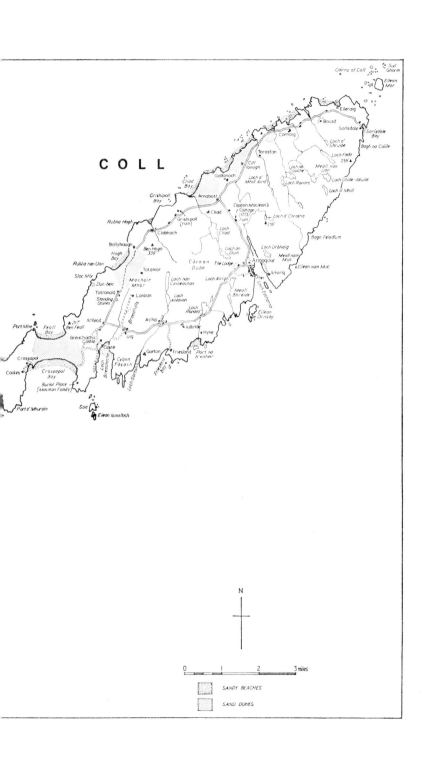

# C O L L

Cairns of Coll
Suil Ghorm
Eilean Mòr
Eileraig
Bousd
Sorisdale
Sorisdale Bay
Bàgh na Coille
Loch a' Ghruibe
Loch Fada 259'
Cornaig
Meall nan Uan
Torastan
Loch na Cloiche
Cill Ionagh
Loch a' Mhill
Gallanach
Loch a' Mhill Aird
Loch Ronard
Loch Guille-caluim
Cliad Bay
Arnabost
Grishipoll Bay
Captain Maclean's
Cottage (1773) ruin
Loch a' Chrotha
Cliad
Bàgh Feisdlum
Rubha Hogh
Grishipoll (ruin)
Loch Cliad
239'
Clabhach
Loch Urbhaig
Meall nam Muic
Ballyhaugh
Ben Hogh 339'
Loch an Duin
Eilean nam Muic
Rubha nan Uan
Hogh Bay
Totamòr
Càrnan Dubh
The Lodge
Arinagour
Sloc Mòr
Machair Mhòr
Loch nan Cinneachan
Loch Airigh
Ativirig
Pier
Dùn beic
Lonban
Loch Anlaimh
Meall Bhrecide
Eilean nam Muic
Totronald
Standing Stones
Breachills
Acha
Loch Ronard
Eilean Orinsay
Port Mòr
Feall Bay
217'
Ben Feall
Arileod
Uig
Kilbride
Hyne
Breachacha Castle
Castle
Cèann Fàsach
Gorton
Friesland
Port na h'eitheir
Crossapol
Loch Breachacha
Loch Gorton
Freshed Bay
Caoles
Crossapol Bay
Burial Place (Maclean Family)
Port a' Mhuráin
Soa
Eilean Iomalloch

N

0    1    2    3 miles

SANDY BEACHES

SAND DUNES

or Canna, terracing continues offshore in the form of reefs, which obstruct ingress. The entrance to the main harbour at Port Mor on the east side is flanked by twin hazards, Bogha Ruadh and Dubh Sgeir, only a few yards apart. The ferry has to meet the mailboat well offshore; so small and low an island gives little protection, and until 1975 there was no call in winter.

Yet Muck is very fertile. Its twenty-four inhabitants run an efficient farming unit, under a tenacious and skilful proprietor. Here island tranquillity may be savoured to the full. Peace washes round the white shores of Gallanach where the old farmhouse, solid and sedate, its walled garden bright with flowers and fruits, recalls childhood pictures of Beatrix Potter's Lakeland farms.

The name Muck, which has long caused amusement, probably derives from *Muc*, the Gaelic for 'pig'. It occurs in other Scottish place-names; Coll has *Meall nam Muc* and *Eilean nam Muc*, north of Loch Eatharna. Maybe Muck was once noted for its pigs—certainly Coll was in the pig business. There are other explanations: the island is shaped like a pig (!); porpoises ('sea-pigs') abound off its coasts; and because it once belonged to the church, the name should be 'Monk'. The latter derivation was adopted (or invented) in the eighteenth century when landlords were known by the name of their property. Boswell's diary, although confusing, brings out the point: 'It was curious to hear the Laird called by his title. "Muck" would not do well, but he was called "Isle of Muck" which went off with great readiness . . . Some call it the "Isle of Monk". The Laird insists on this.'

The island's basalt structure overlies Great Estuarine sediments which outcrop at the foot of 451ft (137m) Beinn Airein on Camas Mor, where agglomerates like Canna 'plumb-pudding' may also be seen. Mural dykes from the volcanoes on Rum and Ardnamurchan traverse the island from north-west to south-east. Between Camas Mor and Port Mor they occur every 20yd on average. East of Port Mor they form walls and trenches, and their serrated tops traverse Camas na

Cairidh on the north coast like decayed saw-teeth. Dykes connect Muck to its north-western outliers Eilean nan Each (Horse Island) and Eagamol. On taller exposures (some exceed 20ft) it is possible to trace the magma flow. Glacial boulder clay covers much land behind Port Mor and the broad slopes above Gallanach, where there is an abundance of blown shell-sand. There are raised beaches at each end of the Port Mor depression, which carries the only road. There is little peat; the only sizeable deposit, on Blar Mor, was stripped long ago.

## COLL

'Col is not properly rocky; it is rather one continued rock, of a surface much diversified with protuberances, and covered with a thin layer of earth, which is often broken and discovers the stone.' Doctor Johnson's 'one continued rock' extends 12 miles from north-east to south-west. It is shaped like a fish, the mouth snapping for a string of north-easterly outliers, the Cairns of Coll, the tail formed by the opposing concavities of Feall and Crossapol Bays. Its greatest width is $3\frac{1}{2}$ miles.

Only around Ben Hogh—339ft (103m), halfway down the north coast—can the protuberances be described as hills. Most of the island is Lewisian gneiss country, low rocky hummocks separated by irregular peat-filled basins, often graced by shallow lochans. Dozens of sandy beaches are wedged between miniature headlands on the north and south-west coasts, but there are none in the bare and uninhabited north-east which looks so uninviting from the Oban car ferry. Island scenery culminates in the elegant sweeping strands at Feall and Crossapol.

Blown sand has helped form several beautiful but limited coastal machair lands and a shore-to-shore strip running from Breachacha to Hogh Bay, some of which is menaced by shifting dunes. A road links the north coast machair to Arinagour on Loch Eatharna, an inlet halfway down the south-east coast, the only passable harbour. Another runs from Arinagour, behind farmhouses on the south-east bays (some served only by footpath) to the Breachacha/Hogh machair strip. Machair grazings supported a considerable dairying industry during the second half of the nineteenth century, and some Collachs are descended from the Kintyre folk brought in to establish it. Modern farming economics have ended dairying and reduced population, now down to 145, most of whom live at Arinagour. A pier to take seagoing ships was at long last provided there in 1967. Although the island is only 7 miles from Mull and 10 from Ardnamurchan, the car ferry runs out from Oban, 54 miles and a minimum of $3\frac{1}{2}$ hours away. There are two island airstrips, and from 1970–5 Coll enjoyed an air service from Glasgow.

Tradition suggests that the name Coll, Gaelic *Colla*, derives from *Cala*, the Gaelic word for harbour, although few mariners would feel Loch Eatharna to merit such commemoration. Another unlikely explanation has the root Norse *kollr*, a high place; but the name is pre-Norse.

Two-thirds of Coll, north of a line from Clabhach to Gorton, is Lewisian gneiss. That normally grey rock is much banded with quartz and other minerals; in the north-west little pink-and-yellow headlands contrast with orange sand and green machair. Seventy basalt dykes cross the bleak shore-line between the north point and Loch Eatharna; others crossing the north-west coast have eroded to form chasms or geos.

The westerly third of the island is made of successive north/south bands: pre-Lewisian calcareous sandstone of immense antiquity metamorphosed into paragneisses containing quartz and marble; Lewisian-age pink orthogneiss; and 'ordinary' Lewisian, less colourful than that in the north-west. The paragneisses have eroded and are largely concealed by sand and peat. A narrow paragneiss band terminates by Gorton shore where the lovely Coll marble outcrops. Pink orthogneiss predominates from Ben Hogh across to Loch Breachacha. Paragneiss underlies the sandy area between Feall and Crossapol Bays, outcropping at their margins—most beautifully so on Ben Feall. The grass-grown ledges of this miniature mountain—it is only 217ft (66m) high—slope dizzily to the sea, and narrow tilted ravines trace marbled slips and stripes. High above the gleaming water springy turf carpets a broad processional way and wraps outcrops like a garment. Finally, the western tip of Coll and part of tidal Gunna are on grey Lewisian, overblown with sand.

All Coll rocks were subjected to crushing which formed semi-vitreous 'flinty crush-rock'. Lustrous veins reticulate in thread-like branches, which differential weathering has carved into bas-relief.

Glaciation occurred from the Mull direction; striae may be seen in the north-west, but glacial drift is rare. Erratics are uncommon. Two prominent lumps of gabbro on the northern flanks of Ben Hogh presumably came from Mull. Both are raised off the ground by smaller rocks. Traditionally they were thrown by a giant and his mistress. Johnson disliked not being able to explain their origin: 'there are so many more important things of which human knowledge can give no account, that it may be forgiven us, if we speculate no longer on two stones in *Col*'.

The island may once have been split by channels running from Cliad to Arinagour, Hogh to Breachacha, and Feall to Crossapol. Raised beaches are widespread up to the 100ft contour in hollows among the rocks, and others must be hidden under peat and blown sand. Examples may be seen in roadside pits from Arinagour to Arnabost, at Grishipol and Loch Cliad. One underlies the peat beds on the Acha road from Arinagour, once a source of fuel for Tiree, and still cut today.

Finally there is blown sand, comminuted shell with high calcareous content. Sand neutralises the acidity of peat and of the poor gneiss soils: hence machair. But it can engulf agricultural land. Boswell wrote of the Hogh Bay area 'the sand has blown of late over a good deal of meadow . . . It is very alarming. People tell that their fathers told them they saw ploughed land over most of the space which is now covered by sand.' Johnson was sceptical: 'I am not of opinion,

31

that by any surveys of landmarks, its limits have ever been fixed.' The use of plants with roots that retain moisture and so bind sand was already known, but difficulty with sandblow continued. The 1871 Ordnance sheet and postwar air cover show that sand has advanced in the last hundred years.

Around Hogh Bay shell carbonate has recrystallised to form strange outcrops and overhangs. Dunes in the Feall–Crossapol 'desert' rise well above 100ft, and great sand-corries are fashioned by the wind into shapes of a rounded beauty so perfect that one hesitates to mar them with footprints.

## TIREE

Tiree is exhilarating. Arriving from any of the other five islands, one wonders at the crowds, the traffic-jam on the pier, the sophistication of signposts, and at an horizon shaped by houses rather than hills. There is a healthy dash of the ordinary and a bracing air of commerce about this thriving community of 865 people.

The island runs 12 miles from north-east to south-west, broadening from 1 mile to 6 miles wide. Much of the coast is scalloped-out into long curving dune-backed surf beaches, where sand-yachts skim and hum like great coloured insects. A fertile machair is in places continuous from coast to coast. Rough Lewisian gneiss occupies each end of the island. The central plain of The Reef is so flat that one may stand close to high water on the eastern coast, and watch the sun dip into the western sea. The south-western end carries two isolated hills: Beinn Hough, 388ft, and Ben Hynish, 460ft. Imposing 200ft cliffs at Ceann a Mhara, the breeding haunt of seabirds, form the south-west tip. Little other ground reaches the 100ft contour. There are five lochs and many lochans—these were more numerous before extensive drainage in the last century.

Most of Tiree is divided into crofts. Croft-houses are scattered widespread over the cultivated land, but there are nucleated villages at Balemartine in the south-west and at

Scarinish, the island metropolis, around a tiny inlet on the eastern coast. Scarinish was the port until 1914, when Gott pier at last freed the people from dependence on a rowing-boat ferry. The car-ferry run from Oban takes four or more hours. A year-round air service operates from Glasgow—a sixty-minute flight to the vast airfield on The Reef, a legacy from World War II. There are many good roads, a few double-tracked.

The name Tiree (Tyree until well into this century; Tiry in the eighteenth) pronounced Tie-ree, may derive from Gaelic *Tir-reidh*, the flat land. Adamnan made the 'reidh' into 'hith' or 'eth' and latinised the name to Ethica Insula. Another explanation would make the root *Tir-I*, the cornland of Iona.

Geology is similar to Coll's—successive bands of gneiss. Pink orthogneiss outcrops beautifully on the Caoles shore, followed by a broad band of grey Lewisian hummocks between coastal machair at Salum and Ruaig. The low neck between Vaul and Gott Bay lies on a band of softer paragneiss. Lewisian then continues, carrying moorland and lochans, until the dead flat Reef is reached—predictably on paragneiss. Tiree marble (pink with green spots) is exposed around Balephetrish and was worked briefly during the 1790s and in Edwardian times. Almost the whole south-west end is on grey Lewisian. Much flinty crush-rock threads the gneiss.

Intruded dykes run along Hough Bay and form serrations across the shore at Baugh. Glacial drift is scanty. Glaciation left erratics, notably the 'ringing-stone' on the coast near Balephetrish, transported from Rum. Afterwards Tiree was probably divided into three islands when the sea washed over the Reef, and from Vaul to Gott Bay.

The Reef's 'river', An Fhaodhail, still threatens to cut the island in two, although 'a barrier of stone and earth' was raised to prevent this in the eighteenth century. An Fhaodhail deposited freshwater alluvium. Much of western Tiree is formed from a 50ft raised beach; other beaches, carrying many lochans, are intercalated into the gneiss behind Scarinish and Ruaig.

Finally there is blown sand, with its history of trouble in the years of overcrowding. In 1771 the improving 5th Duke of Argyll instructed his factor 'to attend to . . . remedies against sand blowing' and warned of 'the pernicious consequence of cuting bent [cutting grasses]', but blowing continued and 'the tenents of several farms were . . . obliged to change the situations of their houses'. Although none of the eighteenth-century village sites was engulfed, and many former sandblow areas are now greened-over, as late as the 1950s Fraser Darling reported 'extensive blow-outs . . . resulting in clearing of dunes . . . down to the iron-stained bedrock'.

Yet blown sand is the basis of Tiree's prosperity, for machair is extensively developed and wind has lifted sand up the flanks of the three 'mountains', converting gneiss soil into fine pasture. Only in the north-east, where there is peat among the rocky hummocks, and in the south-west, where iron pan is exposed at Moss, are there extensive areas of poor land. They amount to barely a third of the island's area—a small fraction indeed in a Hebridean context.

5 Peaks: *(above)* Hallival from Askival in the Coolins of Rum. Coolins of Skye in background *(Douglas Scott)*;
6 *(below)* pitchstone ridge behind An Sgurr of Eigg. Across the Sound, Glen Dibidil and the Rum Coolins *(E. H. Kyme)*

7 Beaches: *(above)* Laig Bay, Eigg. Cleadale and Cuagach townships lie below the Shearwater slopes of Beinn Bhuidhe *(John Currie)*;
8 *(below)* the lonely curve of Crossapol Bay fringed by the sand-mountain country of southern Coll

# 3     SEA AND SKY

'IN north-westerly gales,' says the *West Coast Pilot*, 'the whole area between Skerryvore and Tiree is a mass of breakers, making it impossible to identify the positions of the rocks; this locality should therefore be avoided.'

South Uist lies 24 miles from Canna; Barra Head is 30 miles from Tiree, which is totally exposed from SSE to NNW. Long swells from the Atlantic may roll in to the Sea of the Hebrides for weeks on end, born of very distant winds. The 8th Duke of Argyll described them well when he visited Tiree for the first time:

> When no wind was blowing at all . . . when the surface of the ocean was as calm as the surface of glass or oil, I saw vast *undulations*, in which acres of water were in movement, and which advanced with a silent, majestic motion . . . On meeting shallows, still more in encountering rocks, they at once rose in threatening and rapidly advancing crests, and then broke in furious foam and surge . . .

With strong winds from any exposed quarter massive waves can arise, for the fetch is virtually infinite. According to the Meteorological Office, the Sea of the Hebrides is 'about twice as rough in any given wind as The Minch . . . waves of 30ft have been observed with a south wind of force 7'.

Although the North Atlantic Drift, the tail-end of the Gulf Stream, is rightly credited with the more amiable features of island climate, local water is not particularly warm. Sea temperatures normally vary from 46° F (8° C) in February to a cool 55° F (13° C) in August, but lapses can occur; it is said that a 50ft iceflow was once seen off Tiree in July. Nevertheless the warming effects of the Drift are undeniable. The

c

islands are around 57° N, the latitude of northern Labrador, which enjoys a very different climate.

## SKY

The minister of Small Isles in 1794:

> The air is generally moist, and the weather rainy. The southerly and easterly winds, which are the most frequent, are almost constantly attended with rain . . . The last summer and harvest, 1793, were much more rainy than any remembered, which is all the more singular, as the weather was said to be very dry in the lowlands . . .

The minister of Tiree in the same year:

> Durable frost and snow is very rare . . . yet it may be called a cold climate, in winter, without any shelter . . . When there is frost on the mainland, there is often mild weather on these islands; when snow in the one, there is often but rain on the other . . .

More recently Frank Fraser Darling has remarked on 'high sunshine records of the island of Tiree' and on Canna, 'probably the earliest ground in the whole West Highlands'. These apparently contradictory observations are all true.

A hermit of Glen Martin Muck used to foretell the weather, and Tiree factors took rainfall readings during the nineteenth century, but the first modern observations were made by D. O. Maclean, headmaster of Cornaigmore School, Tiree, from 16 September 1926. 'D.O.' wired his observations three times a day to the Meteorological Office until they set up their own station at the RAF airfield in 1942. A staff of five now keeps continuous watch. A thermometer and rain-gauge in the Lodge grounds on Eigg have been read since 1926. Rainfall records are kept on Muck. In 1957 the Nature Conservancy set up a climatological station at Kinloch and several monthly rain-gauges; work directed by Frank Green, head of their Geographical Sciences Branch, led to a good deal being known of Rum's depressing climate.

*Precipitation*

Most winds reach the islands after blowing over the Atlantic, but that does not necessarily imply a wet climate. Tiree's average annual rainfall is about 44in (112cm), 8in (203mm) less than that for Scotland as a whole. Yet 123in (312cm) a year are recorded in a dark corrie below Barkeval on Rum. Perhaps only climbers and deer (who dislike it) are directly interested in Barkeval's rain, but even at Kinloch on the shores of Loch Scresort the figure is a dampening 99in (251cm). In descending and approximate order of dampness, Eigg and Canna have 60in (152cm) Coll 50 (127cm) and Muck and Tiree 44 (112cm). The wettest month is October and the driest May. Tiree averages 5·1 (12·70cm) and 2·5in (6·32cm) in those months, Eigg 7·2 (18·28cm) and 3·2 (8·09cm), Kinloch, Rum 11·8 (29·83cm) and 5·5 (13·90cm). 'Wet Days' have at least 0·4in (1·27cm). Tiree has about 38 such days in an average year; Coll about 41, and Eigg perhaps 47—London Heathrow has 18. Thunderstorms are uncommon, probably because the islands have little really hot weather. Most thunder occurs in winter. Tiree has snow flurries on perhaps 13 days in an average year, Eigg on 22. On low ground snow may lie for 3 or 4 mornings (10 in Aberdeen and London), but many a late winter dawn sees the Rum Coolins towering white over Laig Bay.

*Mildness*

Winters are mild. In February the isotherm of mean daily maximum temperature 47° F (8° C) runs Tiree–Haverfordwest–Lyme Regis; all places east are colder. December's daily range of temperature is around 6° F (−14° C), similar to that for Isles of Scilly and 4° less than at Heathrow; hence the Dragon's Blood palms in Eigg Lodge grounds. Yet spring arrives late. The May mean daily maximum 55° F (13° C) runs Tiree–Portree–Ullapool–Inverness, all places south being warmer. Summers are cool. The maximum recorded temperature on Tiree was 79° F (26° C), on 2 July 1955. July, the warmest month, has a mean daily maximum around 62° F (17° C), probably less than any low ground in England.

*Wind*

On Sunday 26 February 1961 a south-westerly carried bitter rain and sleet across Tiree's Plain of Reef. In the early afternoon, pressure fell rapidly and the wind, backing to SSE, rose to force 8. As Tiresians took Sunday tea there was a sharp veer to south-west and by 5.40 pm a violent storm, force 11, was hurling hail through the winter night. Ten minutes later the cups on the airfield anemometer jerked the recorder pen to a peak of 101·5 knots, 116mph, the highest wind-speed ever recorded in Great Britain. This famous gust—since exceeded elsewhere—occurred during the passage of an occluded front in an intense depression.

The summer months are relatively calm and the tourist is little affected, but (on average) Tiree experiences force 6 for 10 days in December and force 8 for 66 hours in December–January. The southerly and westerly winds which predominate throughout the year bring changeable weather and the changes can be sudden; on the wettest day there is hope for improvement. Anticyclones over Scandinavia bring dry clear continental air and sparkling days, particularly in spring. Summer easterlies carry warmth, but conditions may be hazy. Winter northerlies bring clear weather, when the islands look their best.

*Sunshine and visibility*

In May Tiree averages over 7·5 hours of bright sunshine per day, a figure exceeding that for Jersey. Coll and Canna probably have around 7 hours, Eigg around 6·5. In June Tiree's 7 hours is equalled only in the coastal fringes from Haverfordwest to Frinton, but by July and August most lowland areas of England have more sun than any of the six islands.

Humidity is high. In June Tiree shows 75 per cent and Eigg 70 per cent, figures comparable with most coastal resorts of England. On the high tops of Rum, humidity is probably little less than 100 per cent for months on end.

Yet island weather is generally bright. The plane from Glasgow may take off into a murky sky, but before Tiree is reached visibility often extends to reveal the islands scattered over a painted sea and the journey may seem all too short. During May–August the likelihood of visibility exceeding 13 miles at 0900 GMT is 53 per cent in Tiree, 41 per cent in Isles of Scilly and 28 per cent in Glasgow.

*Weather contrasts*

The depressions which affect the islands' weather often travel eastwards or north-eastwards between Iceland and Scotland and their diameter is commonly 500–800 miles. London is often in a different weather system, and striking contrasts can arise. In the high summer of 1968 London was sunk in gloom for weeks on end, whilst the islands basked in long sunny days. The sea, creeping in over hot sands, achieved a temperature that tempted even the islanders into the water. The grass turned brown, the burns dried up and by mid-August only two houses on Eigg could draw water from their taps. Hebridean tourism has never looked back from the fillip given by that sensational summer.

*Day-time and day-length*

The islands are in 56°30 N; on 22 June they have 103 minutes more daylight than London. Tiree approaches 7° W and last light comes 84 minutes later than London's.

| | first light | sunrise | sunset | last light | effective day (h.m.) |
|---|---|---|---|---|---|
| 22 *June* | | | | | |
| London | 0354 | 0443 | 2121 | 2200 | 18.06 |
| 56°30′N | 0307 | 0410 | 2153 | 2256 | 19.49 |
| Tiree | 0335 | 0438 | 2221 | 2324 | 19.49 |
| 22 *Dec* | | | | | |
| London | 0723 | 0804 | 1554 | 1635 | 9.12 |
| 56°30′N | 0746 | 0833 | 1524 | 1611 | 8.25 |
| Tiree | 0814 | 0901 | 1552 | 1639 | 8.25 |

# 4 EARLY TIMES AND CLAN TIMES

PREHISTORY

ARLY man probably advanced along coasts rather than through forested and marshy interiors. Around 3000 BC mesolithic people were living in caves near Oban; they may have found their way to the islands, all of which have similar accommodation. Their range of fauna was probably smaller than that on the mainland, and unwanted species could more readily be eliminated. The vast beaches of Coll and Tiree must have been sources of easily gathered food.

On Coll and Tiree virtually every hilltop and headland has its fort; most are now mere shallow hollows, generally circular, surrounded by peripheral mounds reinforced by low irregular lines of grass-grown boulders. The Sgurr of Eigg is said to have been used defensively: the remains of a wall of pitch-stone-column fragments which barred the only approach can still be seen. Another impressive and perhaps more viable fort is Caisteal an Duin Bhan (Castle of the White Hill-fort) near Port Mor Muck where a basalt dyke with overhanging sides has been 'improved' into a stronghold 50 × 30yd (45 × 27m). Its grass-grown top is protceted by a stone rampart 6ft high in places, still more or less continuous; nothing is known of its history. Indeed, with one exception, little is known of any of the islands' forts. They may date from the Iron Age. They may have been used for defence against Vikings. Dun Mor Vaul and a few others on Tiree were circular *brochs*, massive structures of dry-stone walling with inner and outer leaves tied together by rows of stone lintels, which formed the floors of internal galleries.

Lord Colin Campbell excavated Dun Mor Vaul in 1897. A

1962–64 investigation by the Hunterian Museum produced decorated pottery and small tools. Radiocarbon dating distinguished several phases, the first going back to 500 BC, long before the broch was built, when evidence from Vaul and elsewhere suggests that there was a flourishing population on Tiree. They probably came from western France; they cast bronze, kept domestic animals, spun thread and were expert potters. A century or two later another people lived in wattle-and-daub huts on the site. The broch itself dates from the beginning of our era. It was 6oft (20m) in diameter and 25ft (8m) high; the leaves of its circular wall were each 6ft (2m) thick at base, and there was a 3ft (1m) space between them. The ground floor was partly on the living rock, partly of stone-paving in which there was a water-tank. A timber floor 6ft up was supported on stone wall-brackets and timber posts. The skin or thatch roof had a central hole. The broch probably accommodated fifty people in time of danger; it was a communal refuge.

Later a hearth was built and the upper floor removed, suggesting that it had become the home of a single family. Later still the circular wall was reduced to its present height of 6ft, and a new roof was supported on a wall built against the original inner leaf; a fragment of a second-century Roman glass bottle is associated with this phase. There was little evidence of later occupation, but a Viking bone comb was found (perhaps ninth century).

Many forts are traditionally associated with the fairies, who may represent memories of folk other than Gaelic (but not necessarily pre-Gaelic). Only a race of fairies could have occupied the tiny forts on islets in island lochs, often approached by submerged curved causeways. A great deal remains to be learned from archeological investigation.

## GAELS AND CHRISTIANS

The Scots, a Gaelic and nominally Christian people from Ireland, colonised Argyll and the southern Inner Hebrides during the sixth century, calling their new lands Dalriada. Small Isles probably remained under the heathen Picts.

In 563 Columba came to Iona with twelve followers and found the celebrated monastery. In or about 565 his cousin and follower Batheine established another at Campus Lunge Tiree on a site close to Soroby graveyard. Conjecture has linked St Brendan the Voyager with an earlier foundation at Kirkapoll, but Batheine's was probably the first on the island. St Cainnech of Kilkenny may have founded a monastery at Kilkenneth in the western sand country, and St Findchan one at 'Ardcircnis' east of Balephetrish Hill. Columba himself stayed on Tiree; he also went to Skye to convert a Pictish kinglet and may therefore have been on Eigg and Canna. His biographer Adamnan refers to an island called Colossa, the 'home of robbers', probably Coll.

The saint associated with Eigg is Donnan, who may have been a Pict. He trained at Whithorn in Galloway, planned a monastery on Eigg, and asked Columba's blessing. The *Feilire* of Angus, a Culdee priest, tells the story:

> Donnan . . . went to Columcille to make him his soul's friend, upon which Columcille said to him, I shall not be soul's friend to a company of red martyrdom, for thou shalt come to red martyrdom and thy people with thee . . . Donnan then went with his people to the Hebrides and they took up their abode there in a place where the sheep of the Queen of the country were kept. *Let them be killed* said she. *But that would not be a religious act* said her people. But they were murderously assailed . . .

The massacre is referred to in Marion Gorman's *Calendar*: 'Donnan the great, with his monks. Fifty-two were his congregation. There came pirates of the sea and slew them all. Eig is the name of that island'; and with brutal terseness in the *Annals* of Tighernach for 617: 'Combustio Donnain—Eiga'.

Columba died in 595. If Tighernach's date is correct Donnan's monastery was established twenty years before the massacre; but Angus's account infers that his stay on Eigg was as short as the queen's temper. The fort at Rubha na Crannaig on the shore of Poll nam Partan shows signs of secondary occupation suggestive of early Christian cells. Perhaps St Donnan was there; the nearby hamlet is called Kildonnan. St Donnan's day, 17 April, was an Eigg holiday into the nineteenth century. None of the islands' ruined 'pre-Reformation' chapels date from Columban times—early monasteries were probably wattle-and-daub.

Vikings burned Soroby in 672, but religious life on the islands continued. There was a priest on Rum in 677—appropriately named Beccan the Solitary—perhaps at Papadil (although the name is Norse) or at Kilmory. Oan Abbott of Eigg died in 724, when the Irish Annals list four former incumbents. An Abbot of Soroby died in 774. The island monasteries probably succumbed to Viking raids around the end of the eighth century.

### VIKINGS

The peasant lost his land and life
Who dared to bide the Norseman's strife
The hungry battle-birds were filled
In Skye with blood of foeman killed
And wolves on Tiree's lonely shore
Dyed red their hoary jaws with gore . . .

Bjorn Cripplehand's verse records the dangerous years when Vikings were mere raiders. Later they colonised some or all of the six islands. In 985 Earl Sigurd of Orkney sent Kari to collect taxes from Earl Gilli of Coll. Gilli (the name is Gaelic) was still there early in 1014, having just returned from spending Christmas on Orkney. He has been associated with Cnoc Ghillebreidhe, a hill east of Gallanach where 'ancient walls' were still visible at the beginning of this century and a 'noble family' traditionally lived. In 1016 Olaf the Thick—afterwards King of Norway—sailed to Grislopolla 'fought there with Vikings' and went to 'Seliopolla and there gave battle [at] a castle . . . known as Gunnvallsborg'. Was 'Grislopolla' Grishipoll on Coll, 'Seliopolla' Heylipoll on

Tiree, and 'Gunnvallsborg' the fort on Gunna? Magnus Barelegs, a kilted king, harried Tiree in 1098 during a successful bid to re-assert authority over the Hebrides, but on his death five years later control passed to the kings of Man. In 1123 the Manx King Godfrey made his son Reginald ruler of an area which seems to have included Coll and Tiree; an Irish poem refers to 'Reginald King of Coll' about the same time.

Skeletons of men and horses 'completely armed' found during the eighteenth century at Cornaigbeg Tiree have been attributed to Viking times. A few Viking artifacts are preserved. A magnificent sword-hilt of gilded bronze inlaid with silver plates and wires, bearing circles and scrolls of black niello, was recovered when a field at Kildonnan Eigg was levelled-down in 1830. (The place was called *Dail Sithean*, Field of the Fairy Knolls, and the islanders were reluctant to work there.) In 1875 a deliberate dig opened the two Viking burial mounds near Kildonnan House; grave-goods included sword-blades, an axe-head, a sickle and belt-clasp of iron and a bronze penannular thistle-brooch of the tenth century. A fine Norwegian 'tortoise' brooch in bronze and silver wire was found on Tiree in 1872, and another on Coll after a storm in December 1879 had removed much sand around Gallanach. Viking women used a pair of brooches to attach pinafore-dress to bodice; perhaps the Gallanach brooch belonged to one of Earl Gilli's camp-followers. These objects may be seen at the National Museum of Antiquities in Edinburgh.

The largest Viking relic on the islands is a ship-burial at Rubha Langan-innis, Canna. Nothing in the wild history of the islands can compare with the savage spectacular of a ship-burial, when Viking warriors paraded and caroused amidst smoke and flames from the burning galley bearing the body of their chief. Perhaps the quasi-military organisation of old island funerals, with their relays of coffin-bearers and men shouldering-arms with spades and the whisky-born wakes that followed date from Viking times.

There is (or was) a Coll tradition that in 1384 Maclean of Duart aided by thirty men under a redoubtable old lady from Caoles expelled the last three Norse chiefs in all the Hebrides from the forts at Dun Beic Totronald, Dun Dubh Grishipoll and Loch na Cinneachan (of the Gentiles). The date of their expulsion was arrived at quite simply. The Macleans of Coll sold the island in 1856. According to their (lost!) records it was in Maclean hands for 472 years; deduct one figure from the other. Because 1384 is 118 years after the Treaty of Perth by which Norway ceded the Hebrides to the Scottish crown, the story has been subjected to scholarly ridicule. Yet there could be something in it. After the Perth treaty Norse residents became the subordinate race; and racial tension is not an invention of the twentieth century.

### LORDS OF THE ISLES

During the twelfth century Somerled MacGillebride led a Gaelic underground movement directed against the Manx and Scottish crowns, established himself on the Argyll mainland and made his son Dougall 'king' of an area which included Coll and Tiree. When Somerled was killed in 1164 his sons acquired the Inner Hebrides: Reginald had Islay; Dougall Mull, Coll and Tiree, and Angus Skye and Small Isles. In the next generation Islay went to Reginald's son, Donald; Mull, Coll and Tiree to Dougall's son, Duncan, and Skye and Small Isles to Reginald's son, Ruari. Three island clans thus emerge: MacDonalds, MacDougalls of Lorne and MacRuaris of Garmoran (which stretched from Ardnamurchan to the Uists).

During the thirteenth century the Scottish crown began its attempts to control the Hebrides, a process which was to take half a millennium. In 1262 a royal force 'sacked villages and desecrated churches' on Skye and Small Isles, and 'in wanton fury raised children on the points of their spears and shook them until they fell to the ground'. The MacRuaris called for Norse help, and in 1263 Haakon II's great fleet sailed south. MacRuaris and MacDonalds supported this final and fatal attempt to assert Norwegian power, but after Largs Alexander III of Scotland generously confirmed them in their lands.

The clans took divergent lines during the Scottish Wars of Independence. The MacDougalls backed Balliol. The MacRuaris supported Bruce, who married into the family and may have hidden in Garmoran when, as Robert I, he fled from the mainland in the winter of 1306 (perhaps he went to Small Isles—all their caves have spiders). The canny MacDonalds supported Balliol, Bruce and England as occasion offered, contriving to be on the winning side at Bannockburn, when Angus Og MacDonald led 5,000 tribesmen in the final charge. He acquired much MacDougall land, including Coll and Tiree.

Angus Og's son and successor John of Islay married Amy, sister to MacRuari of Garmoran. When MacRuari was murdered in 1346 Amy inherited the Garmoran lands which thus passed to her husband; John MacDonald's writ then ran from Islay to Lewis and from Glencoe to Barra. Soon afterwards John divorced her to make a glittering marriage with Margaret, daughter of Robert the High Steward, later King Robert II. He could then afford to be magnanimous to his former enemies: by a settlement of 1354 he returned Coll to the MacDougalls 'for ever' and made them Baillies of Tiree, where they could keep eight sixteen-oared galleys. On the settlement document John MacDonald styled himself *Dominus Insularum*, Lord of the Isles. For the first and last time there was Home Rule in the Hebrides; although constantly threatened, it lasted for 144 years.

### The Clanranalds on Small Isles

John 1st Lord of the Isles had two sons by Amy MacRuari: Ranald and Godfrey. By his second wife, Princess Margaret, he had three, of whom the eldest was Donald. A political swindle was mounted by which, on John's death, Donald was to inherit all his father's lands and succeed as Lord of the

48

Isles; Ranald would have only the former MacRuari lands as a vassal of Donald and his heirs. These arrangements were confirmed by royal charters in 1363 and 1373.

On John's death in 1386 Donald MacDonald was installed 2nd Lord:

> Ranald . . . called a meeting of all the nobles of the Islands and his brethren . . . and gave the sceptre to his brother at Cill Donnan on Eigg who was nominated MacDonald and Donald of Isla, contrary to the opinion of the men of the Islands . . . Donald took the Lordship with the consent of his brethren and the nobles of the Islands, all other persons being obedient to him.

The Clanranalds owned Eigg for 440 years.

*The Duart Macleans on Tiree and Coll*

The Macleans are the sons of Gille-ain, Mac-Gilleains, Macleans. Gille-ain followed MacDougall in the Wars of Independence, and his sons Hector and Lachlan negotiated the MacDonald/MacDougall settlement of 1354. According to Maclean tradition they later bullied the 1st Lord into granting them land; it seems an unlikely tale, but Lachlan became successively the 1st Lord's son-in-law, Chamberlain, and Constable of Duart Castle on the Sound of Mull. He acquired land in Mull and Morvern, continued as Chamberlain to the 2nd Lord, and was presumably master of ceremonies at the Eigg investiture of 1386. (His decendant, who lives today at Duart, is Charles Hector Fitzroy Maclean, 1st Baron and 11th Baronet of Maclean and Morvern, 27th Chief of Clan Maclean—and Lord Chamberlain of the Household to Queen Elizabeth II.)

Despite the 1354 settlement the MacDougalls cease to be mentioned in the fragmentary records. In 1390 the 2nd Lord made Lachlan Baillie of Coll and Tiree, and feudal landlord of Heylipoll and Mannal in the latter island. Ownership of the rest of Tiree seems to have been disputed between Lachland's descendants, the Duarts, and his brother's, the Lochbuies, until the sixteenth century. Lachlan also became

Constable of Cairnburgh Castle in the Treshnish. For the sustenance of the garrison on that barren rock he was entitled to 'victual meal and cheese' which in 1409 he commuted for ownership of the south-west end of Coll (perhaps less sandy than it is now). It is not clear who held the rest of the island.

## Coll Macleans

One stormy day in October 1773 Boswell fell to rummaging among papers at Breachacha New Castle:

> The first Maclean of Coll was a younger son of the family of Maclean. His father gave him the middle part of Coll as his patrimony but made it the jointure lands of Lady Maclean. MacNeill of Barra married her and came and lived in Coll. Young Coll was so impatient to get possession that he got some of the clan to assist him against MacNeill . . .

'Young Coll' was John Garbh, 1st Maclean of Coll. His impatience is understandable. He is said to have had a Lord of the Isles' charter to 'Coll' in 1431; James II granted or confirmed him in 'lands in' the island in 1449; but his father, Lachlan Bronnach 7th of Duart, died after 1467. The Duarts seem to have kept the two ends of the island.

According to tradition John Garbh invaded Coll with one follower, Gille Riabhach, the hero of the battle of Grishipoll Burn between MacNeill's men and loyal islanders. Hard-pressed by a fearsome character called the 'Black Tailor of the Axe' the Gille retreated step by step until his back was to the burn; as the Tailor's axe swooped down upon him he leaped 13ft backwards to the opposite bank. The Tailor was dumbfounded (as well he might be) and, thrown off balance, his axe flew from his hand. The Gillie caught it, leaped back, and split the skulls of the Tailor and MacNeill. MacNeill's men retreated successively to MacNeill's Bay, Gunna, and Port Chuan Neil, Tiree, where they were routed.

There is economy in Gaelic tradition. At Ceann a Mhara, Tiree, a 15ft chasm separates coastal cliffs from an offshore island. It seems that a Tiree man, pursued by an ox (not an axe!), rounded on the animal at the cliff-top. When it still came on he escaped by leaping backwards across the chasm which is still called *Sloc a Chain,* 'Gully of the Leap'—and there is a similar story from Mull.

The Coll Macleans acquired Rum. By Eigg tradition Clanranald exchanged it for Coll's 'great galley', but regretted the deal when the vessel's timbers proved rotten. That may explain an uncertainty in the Coll tale: 'Clanranald *for some reason* . . . refused to confirm the sale. John Garbh carried him prisoner to his castle at Breachacha where he detained him for nine months, when the right of disputed succession was fully conceded.' James II (1437–60) is said to have confirmed the Coll's ownership of Rum, but the first extant reference is in 1528. An account of 1549 states that Rum 'perteins to the Laird of Coll' but 'obeyis to McGillane of Doward instantlie'. Around 1580 it 'pertains to ane Barron callit the Laird of Challow . . . but is possest and in the hands of Clanranald'.

### REBELS ON EIGG

The Scottish crown forced the 4th Lord of the Isles to forfeit the Hebrides in 1498, but was itself unable to exercise effective control and a power vacuum lasted into the seventeenth century.

In 1543 Donald Dubh MacDonald (a descendant of the Island Lords) escaped from a royal dungeon, fled to Eigg and held conference there with the western chiefs, including Clanranald and the two Macleans. They acknowledged him Lord of the Isles. He appointed Commissioners with startling terms of reference:

> We Donald Lord of ye Isles . . . with adviss and consent of air barronis and counseill of ye Ilis . . . giffard our full power express bidding and command to . . . all and haill ye saidis Commissionaris . . . and in special testifying our Landis instantlie be maid to ane nobill and potent prince Harye ye Acht

The Commissioners met King Henry, 1,300 crowns of Tudor gold changed hands, but the Hebrides stayed Scottish.

Eigg saw the last MacDonald rebellion, led in 1615 by Sir James MacDonald of Islay, another of the Lords' descendants. Sentenced to death for alleged rebellious activities, he escaped from Edinburgh and reached Sleat of Skye. Government was in a panic; £5,000 was offered for him, dead or alive. Harbours were watched and warships diverted. In the second week of June Sir James and 150 followers landed on Eigg and were joined by a gang of dispossessed MacDonalds led by Coll Keitach, back from a pirating trip to St Kilda. There was quite a jamboree:

> Sir James and his company stood in one place by themselves, where [Coll Keitach] with his company went round about him, once; and at the next about saluted him with a volley of shots; and continued so shooting and inuiring of him for half an hour; and thereafter came to every man, chapping hands.

Men from Clan Ian, then occupying Muck and Canna, also joined the band. Having commandeered cattle from Eigg and Rum the rebels sailed south, to ultimate defeat. Coll Keitach changed sides and was pardoned. Sir James escaped, but later returned to live in London—a prosaic enough end for the last aspirant to the Island Lordship.

### FEUD ON COLL AND TIREE

Because no one's writ ran among the Hebrides, and religious restraint was weakened by the absence of Presbyterian ministers after the 1560 Reformation, feuding became widespread and ruthless.

The Islay MacDonalds invaded Tiree in 1562, and in 1578 'put to death all the inhabitants that fell into their hands, as well as the domestic animals'. Coll also suffered MacDonald invasion in 1562, but most of that island's troubles arose from feuds between Duarts and Colls. In 1537 the Duarts kidnapped Hector 5th of Coll, who traditionally obtained release by charming his gaoler with songs of his own

9 Houses: *(above)* Main Street, Arinagour, Coll, 1929 *(Violet Banks)*;
10 *(below)* cottage of the old style at Salum, Tiree

11 Different styles: *(above)* the new castle from the old in Coll;
12 *(below)* the Lodge, Eigg*(P. Brian Swain)*

composition. A Duart invasion in 1561 may have been an attempt to regain ownership of the two ends of the island (lost to the Church before the Reformation). After the Colls backed an abortive Duart 'Palace Revolution' of 1577–8, the Duarts were on Coll again, and the Tutor of Duart was beheaded at Breachacha.

Tradition recalls a Duart invasion in 1593, which took place on the death of Hector Roy 6th of Coll. His heir was a boy living on the mainland and the head man on Coll was Neil Mor Maclean. When the Duart ships approached, the people were following their chief's funeral procession; women were left to complete the obsequies as the island rallying-cry rang out. Line of battle was formed at Totronald. Time was short and the Colls' flag was forgotten; consternation reigned until an old man stepped forward, snatched off his blue bonnet and cried, 'Let my bald head be your banner and you will not go back today!' Neither did they. The Duarts were vanquished. By sunset the burn that trickles south from the Machair Mor to Breachacha was choked with their heads, and ducks swam around in their blood. The strict veracity of this account is proved by the name ever since given to the burn: Struthan nan Ceann (Stream of the Heads).

When the Duarts later subdued the island, Neil Mor went underground, but was betrayed and killed. The young Coll chief successfully petitioned the Privy Council and in 1596 was restored to his estate. The four men who betrayed Neil Mor were hanged on Cnoc a Chrocaine (Hangman's Hill), Breachacha. There is proof of this story too; four skeletons were found there in 1896.

### EIGG CAVE MASSACRE

*Uamh Fhraing*, the Cave of St Francis or the Ribbed Cave, called the Cave of Tears in Victorian times, faces the sea across a raised beach on Eigg's lonely south coast. Formed by wave action on a fault in the basalt, it is low and narrow for the first yard or two beyond its mouth; entering involves a scramble on the muddy floor. Inside there is thick darkness. As one's eyes adjust, the place is seen to resemble a roughly excavated tunnel, rising into murky distance. It is quite roomy, perhaps 200ft (60m) long and 20ft (6m) wide.

A book could be (and is being) written on the ramifications of the Eigg Cave Massacre. Here there is space only for an outline of the 'mainstream' story. Because MacDonalds occupied land on Skye claimed by the MacLeods of Harris, there was feuding between the two clans; Eigg's Clanranald MacDonalds became involved. In March 1577 bad weather forced a MacLeod boat to put into Eigg. The crew asked politely for food, were refused, taken prisoner and cast adrift with their hands chopped off (MacLeod version). They raped some island girls and were told to leave (Clanranald). Alastair Crotach, 8th MacLeod of Harris, sailed for Eigg with a large force, vowing vengeance. All but one of the 396 islanders hid in Uamh Fhraing. The MacLeods landed, burned houses, destroyed food and crops, and searched for the people; they found only an old lady hiding in a cave at Singing Sands. They spared her, ploughed up Laig beach to prevent her harvesting the spout-fish (!) and set sail for home. But as they were leaving they spotted a scout sent out from the cave. They turned back . . . Snow was lying, and the sagacious scout returned to the cave walking backwards. Despite that subtle ploy the MacLeods found Uamh Fhraing, lit a fire at its mouth and suffocated all those inside. (Years later the MacDonalds took revenge by burning a church-full of Mac-Leods—less one old lady.)

There are obvious objections to this unlikely story. Could 395 people have reached the cave before the MacLeods saw them? Would they not have left tracks? It must have taken a day or more for the MacLeods to search and ravage the island; might lack of oxygen or excess carbon dioxide have caused the folk in the cave to suffocate themselves? When the scout reported that he had been seen (and that snow was lying) surely the people would have left the cave rather than face a certainty of being trapped? Similar stories are told of

Coll and Ardnamurchan . . . Alastair Crotach was dead long before 1577 . . .

And there are other difficulties. In 1588, according to Privy Council papers, Sir Lachlan MacLean of Duart

> accompanyed with a grite nawmer of thevis broken men, and sornars of Clannis, besydis the nawmer of ane hundred Spanyeartis, come, bodin in fear of weir, to his Majesteis proper ilis of Canna Rum Eg and the Isle of Elennole [Muck] and, after they had scorned, wracked and spoilled the saidis hail Illis, they treassonablie raised fyre and in maist barborous, shameful and creull maner, brynt the same Illis, with the haill men, weimen and childrene being thairintill, not spairing the pupillis and infantis . . . The like barbarous and shameful crueltie has sendle been herd of amangis Christeanis in ony kingdome of age . . .

(The Spaniards were from the Armada ship that sank in Tobermory Harbour.) Sir Lachlan was 'incarcerat in Castro de Edinburghe'. Were there *two* massacres on Eigg in eleven years?

In 1625 a Catholic mission came to the island (see p 170) and 'converted' 198 people. If either massacre took place everyone over the age of forty-eight must have been an 'incomer'; but the chatty mission reports are silent on the subject. Yet human skeletons were present in the cave, according to the story told to Boswell in 1773; were reported by the parish minister in 1794, and seen by Walter Scott in 1814 and Hugh Miller in 1845. By 1854 they had been collected and buried—no one knows where. The most sensible remark ever made about the massacre came from a Free Church minister of Eigg: 'the less I enquired into its history . . . the more I was likely to feel I knew something about it'.

### EARLY WRITTEN ACCOUNTS

Donald Munro Dean of the Isles wrote an *Account* of the islands in 1549 (Appendix B). An anonymous *Description* of around 1580 was probably produced for James VI who had notions of colonising the Hebrides. Although neither author would have wished to paint too unattractive a picture, both *Account* and *Description* are salutary reminders that ordinary life went on, despite feuding (subsequently over-emphasised by romanticism). The *Description* lists 'men raised to the weiris'. 'Eg . . . fertile in corn and bestiall' had 60. 'Romb . . . an isle of small profit' had only 7. Canna had 20, Muck 16, 'Collow' ('very fertile . . . sum little birkinn woodis') had 140. 'Tierhie', with 300, was 'commodious and fertile of corns and store of gudes . . . all teillit land' and its lucky landlord was 'great McClane of Doward'.

Eighty years later Duart's Tiree rent-roll was £10,000 Scots (perhaps £500 sterling) paid mostly in kind. Each of twenty 'Tirungs' paid 40 bolls (cwt) of oatmeal, 12 stones of cheese, 12 quarts of butter, 16 wedders, '4 dussan of pultrie with eggs', four loads of peat, a cow at Martinmas and a cow and calf at Whitsunday. Eight weavers each paid a merk (67p). The whole island paid 60 ells of linen and 'a saill and hair taikle to a galey', and 'the Falconers had free quarters and Lambes . . . for the haulks'. The last entry in this 1662 rental, which is (or was) in the 'Argyll charter chest', throws a startling light on life in clan times: 'Tirie was wont to quarter all the gentlemen men that waited on McLean all winter, *not under a 100.*'

# 5   CAMPBELLS AND JACOBITES

URING the seventeenth century, government—still lacking the power to control the Hebrides—turned to using Clan Campbell as its agent. Campbell wealth and power increased at the expense of island clans like the Macleans and Clanranalds. The Campbell chiefs, *MacCalain Mor*, sons of Great Calum, became Lieutenants of the Isles, Heritable Justice-Generals of Argyll and the Isles, Admirals of the Western Coasts, Lords of Lorne and Earls and Dukes of Argyll. The Macleans and Clanranalds countered by supporting any cause that might curb Campbell power: Montrose and Charles I in the Civil War when the Campbells backed the Commonwealth; James II in the 1688 Revolution when the Campbells backed William of Orange; the Old and the Young Pretenders when the Campbells backed the House of Hanover. The Campbells backed winners.

## DOWNFALL OF THE DUARTS

Over the years Duart power was sapped by feuds; fines for outrages like the 1588 affair against Small Isles; early deaths of successive chiefs; support of the losers in the Civil War and by debts—which the Argylls bought—resulting from those mistakes and misfortunes. In 1672 the 9th Earl as principal creditor (and Justice-General) successfully claimed the entire Duart rental. When the tenants refused to pay he sent letters of ejection (32 on Tiree, 2 on each end of Coll, 1 on Gunna) which they ignored. In 1674 he attempted to arrest the defaulters; a private war broke out and Maclean of Brolass, Duart leader during the minority of the chief, garrisoned Cairnburgh.

The Earl managed to install his own Baillie on Tiree, one Lachlan Maclean, whose brief and troubled term of office came to an end when in 1675 Brolass landed at Scarinish

> with twenty-four men in armes . . . [and] violently carried away . . . cornes, bear, horses and swyne . . . oppresses the tenents . . . and caused them to bring in meall and all other sorts of provisione, expelling Lauchlane M'Lean Balzie [from] his house in Kelipoll.

Lachlan and his family fled to Coll where (he wrote to the Earl in 1676) they were 'famished' and subjected to 'savage cruelties'.

Clearly the Argyll writ did not yet run on Tiree and Coll. Three years later, however, the Earl brought out the 'western militia' (ie received direct government support) and successfully invested Breachacha Castle. Hector Roy 10th of Coll was fighting as a mercenary in Holland. His brother, Donald, marched out of Breachacha at sunset on 2 July 1679, delivered up all 'guns and halberts' and undertook to become Argyll's 'obedient subject'. Thereafter the Colls trimmed to the Campbell wind.

Cairnburgh fell on 7 July. Tiree, whose only defensive work was a tiny castle on the island in Loch an Eilean (see p 189), passed to the Argylls, with the ends of Coll and the rest of the Duart estates. In the following year Charles II urged his Privy Council to purchase Tiree for young Duart, to give him a respectable income. The Council refused, but asked Argyll to pay an equivalent annuity (he didn't). Argyll later over-reached himself by mounting an unsuccessful coup in favour of Monmouth, and forfeited his lands; but his son, the 10th Earl, who supported William or Orange in 1688, regained them and was promoted Duke. Men from Tiree and Coll supported Duart and King James's cause at Killiecrankie, but it all came to nothing and in 1692 Duart went into exile. At the beginning of the present century, Tiresians, when asked who owned their island, would answer '*the Macleans* —but the Duke has it now'.

Early in the seventeenth century Campbell pressure caused the MacIans of Ardnamurchan to occupy Canna and Muck—Clanranald territory acquired by the Church (see p 52). In 1617 the Bishop of the Isles sold Muck to Lachlan 7th of Coll who promptly expelled the MacIan squatters. Fourteen went to court at Inverary and several were executed. Lachlan made the island over to his second son, Hector, 1st Maclean of Muck, who was murdered in 1625 when complete Campbell occupation of Ardnamurchan reduced the MacIans to lifting his cattle.

Around 1627 Argyll acquired the superiority of Eigg and Canna—ie bullied the Clanranalds into paying him for the right to their own land. In 1672 they paid £700 a year and a galley of sixteen oars for thirty days 'in the seas between Canna and Iona', and in 1696 the 1st Duke granted Lieutenant Daniel Calder, of his Argyll Militia, a 'factory . . . to uplift the rents'. Perhaps as a result of such impositions the Clanranalds put Eigg in pawn; by 1715 the tenants were paying rent to Macleod of Talisker. The Argylls were still superiors of Eigg in 1780, and of Rum in 1768.

### A CASE OF THE SECOND SIGHT

One Sunday in 1685, after Father O'Rain's service at Kildonnan, an Eigg seer addressed the congregation:

> *they should all flit* . . . people of strange and different habits and arms were to come . . . to use all acts of hostility, as killing, burning, tirling and deforcing of women . . . [He had] . . . seen an apparition of a man in a red coat lined with blue and . . . a strange sort of blue cap with a very high cock . . . kissing a comely maid of Kildonnan . . . a man in such a dress would certainly debauch . . . such a young woman.

The 1688 Revolution made this forecast less fanciful on a Catholic island and a few families left. The story spread; it was common knowledge in Edinburgh and was heard by John Fraser, minister of Tiree, who was collecting such tales for his *Deuteroscopia.*

In 1689 the sloops *Lamb* and *Dartmouth* carrying 600 Cameronians under Major James Ferguson were sent north to overawe the adherents of the exiled James II. That summer Ferguson removed John Fraser from Tiree—he had Episcopalian tendencies unsuited to the strictly Presbyterian climate which followed the Revolution—and the minister became an involuntary passenger on *Dartmouth.* She put into Armadale, Skye, where an Eigg boat's crew, who happened to be ashore, killed one of the Cameronians in a brawl. *Dartmouth,* with John Fraser still aboard, sailed for Eigg. The Cameronians landed, wearing their red coats lined with blue and their high-cocked hats . . . Ferguson was 'sufficiently revenged' on the islanders and a Kildonnan girl was raped. The lass subsequently married an islander, 'her misfortune being pitied, and not reckoned her crime'.

## THE '45

Towards noon on 25 July 1745 the French light frigate *Du Teillay* rounded the south of Eigg and by early afternoon had cleared the Sound of Arisaig, on passage from Eriskay to Loch nan Uamh. She carried Charles Edward Stuart.

Maclean of Duart was detained in Edinburgh on well-founded suspicion of being in French service. Ranald 17th of Clanranald, an old man 'given to the bottle', was restrained by his businesslike half-brother, MacDonald of Boisdale, but his Catholic son 'Young Clanranald' was among the gentry who met the Prince. They were apprehensive at Duart's arrest and depressed by the absence of French support, but Charles had a persuasive tongue and on 6 August *Du Teillay* sailed back through the Sound, leaving her royal passenger behind. Many Eigg and Canna men served—traditionally under John MacDonald of Laig—in Young Clanranald's regiment, voluntarily or otherwise. Their exploits live in history.

Hector 13th of Coll was a substantial citizen (he later built Breachacha New Castle) anxious to prove his loyalty to King George. During the summer Sir Alexander MacDonald wrote to Lord President Forbes 'Mr Maclean of Coll . . . assures us of his own wisdom; and as he has mostly the direction of that clan promises . . . to prevent their being led astray'. Hector had sixty Collachs 'volunteer' for the Argyll Militia— a body commanded by Colonel Jack Campbell, later 5th Duke. He fitted them out with uniforms and shipped them to Inveraray at his own expense; but government failed to supply arms and they returned home.

Not a man could be found for the militia on Argyll's Tiree. Many tried to join the Prince but only four succeeded, for the navy was patrolling the island seas and staving-in boats. Tiresians relieved their frustration by threatening Factor Campbell of Barnacarry 'in such a manner that he had reason to make the best of his way' off the island, which was 'constantly on the flutter'.

## THE '46

On 3 April 1746 a naval vessel put into Canna. Twenty cows were demanded:

> the flower of the islanders was still with the Prince; so that the Bailie judged it safer to grant [the] request . . . But being wind-bound for 4 days . . . behold! they complained . . . the beef of the cattle slaughtered stunk, and [demanded] the same number over again. The Bailie reckoned this . . . unjust . . . Upon which the officer . . . gathers all the cattle of the island . . . shot 60 of the best dead, threw the old beef overboard and would not allow the poor distressed owners to finger a gobbet of it, no, not a single tripe.

On the 18th, King George's men were hunting the Canna women, who were reduced to hiding 'in grottos and the hollows of hideous precipices'. They went after a pregnant woman of fifty. Having fettered her husband '12 of them was at her heels when she . . . sinking down into the very depth of a quagmire, they leaps over her believing she was still before them. The poor woman contented herself to continue there all the night.' She aborted and died.

On 20 May, Boisdale talked the fugitive Prince out of establishing royal headquarters on Eigg. Did Young Clanranald visit the island in connection with that crazy notion? Was he concealed in the cave at the north point, now known as Clanranald's? Tradition knows nothing of the first question, but answers the second with a confident affirmative. However, it is known that Captain John MacDonald of Kinlochmoidart, one of Clanranald's officers, was on Eigg towards the end of May and that he hid in a cave when, on the 30th, Captain John Ferguson brought HMS *Furnace* into the harbour and 100 men came ashore to collect arms. Few were forthcoming. When a search was ordered the parish minister, Donald McQueen, advised MacDonald to surrender, which he did. Ferguson promised him 'full protection'.

> Mr McQueen [then] advises MacDonald to send for the men with the remainder of their arms . . . some dozen of lads . . . were seen coming in a body. Immediately Ferguson ordered MacDonald to be seized . . . the men laid down their arms . . . MacDonald was . . . stript . . . there was a devilish paper found about him, *containing a list of all the Eigg folk that were in the Prince's service*. Then that catalogue was read by their patronimicks in the name of giving protection, which ilk one answered cheerfully, and was drawn out into another rank, so that there were no fewer than 38 snatched aboard . . . most of them was marryed men, leaving throng families.

The names of twenty-seven are known. Angus M'Donald, farmer at Grulin: transported. John M'Donald, farmer at Howlin: transported. Roderick M'Donald, farmer at Kirktown: transported. John M'Dougall, pedlar of Galnashel: transported. John M'Lean, gardener at Laagg: transported. Donald M'Donald, farmer at Fivepenny, taken upon suspicion but never was in the Rebellion: transported all the same . . .

Having slaughtered cattle, burnt houses and 'ravished a girl or two', Ferguson sailed for Tobermory where the prisoners were transferred to a tender. On 15 June he returned to Eigg; maybe there had been wind of the Prince's notion to set up there. Nothing being found, he went over to Canna to pick up the Baillie.

Charles Edward left Loch nan Uamh for France on 20 September. During November some French privateers, still seeking to rescue him, put into Eigg. They were told he had gone. Who wished him back again?

The Eigg prisoners went north-about Scotland to hulks at Inverness or on the Thames. Those still alive were 'tried'. Two were released. The rest died in Barbados. Captain MacDonald was released and returned to Kinlochmoidart where he lived for many years with his conscience. Captain Ferguson was praised by Cumberland for 'diligence and good conduct' and rose to command a line-of-battle ship. James MacDonald Baillie of Canna survived to tell the story of Eigg and Canna in the '46 to his kinsman the great Gaelic poet, Alastair MacDonald, whose descriptions have been used in this brief account.

### COLL AND TIREE

Factor Campbell of Barnacarry returned to Tiree in July 1746 with a detachment of militia and orders to burn some houses—odd instruction for a landlord's agent.

According to a Tiree tradition, Neil MacFadyen and Donald MacLean Ruaig were hijacked on to a 'French brig' and forced to pilot her into Loch nan Uamh to collect the fugitive Prince. They escaped by launching the brig's dinghy under fire as she passed Coll with the Prince on board: when they got ashore Hector of Coll confiscated the dinghy and sent them back to Tiree. Neil disappears from the tale. Donald hid in a Vaul cave and finally expiated his involuntary sin by joining King George's army.

Hector himself was demonstratively loyal. Imagine his embarrassment when troops on disarming duty ('just a routine check') uncovered a consignment of arms, clearly destined for the Prince, on Coll. He had to write a most difficult letter to General Campbell, the future 4th Duke, currently in charge of Hebridean operations. It appeared that his brother Lachlan —who married a daughter of Brolass, Duart leader in the 'private war'—received the arms from 'an Irish officer'. Lachlan was 'a wild man, a very idle odd character, *and a poet*'. He would be disinherited. A receipt for the arms is still preserved at Breachacha Castle, but the sceptical general ordered Coll's boats to be stove-in.

Hector died childless and the estate passed to Hugh, a brother younger than Lachlan.

# 6    DISASTROUS IMPROVEMENT

THE population of the six islands was perhaps 3,500 in 1745. In 1821 it peaked at 7,065 (graphs 1–3). This rapid growth led to gross overcrowding now difficult to imagine. It had several causes. Potato-growing spread after 1743, when Old Clanranald brought seed from Irish estates. Potatoes suited the climate and, grown in conjunction with traditional cereals, eliminated monocultural famine. They prevented scurvy. Drainage reduced malaria. Inoculation curbed smallpox, rife in the previous century and after the '45. In 1756 there were 105 cases on Tiree, many fatal; during the 1770s Dr MacAskill of Skye was inoculating at half-a-crown a head with a mere 1 per cent fatality-rate, and Maclean of Muck had eighty of his people treated. There were three courses of inoculation on Coll and Tiree between 1778 and 1794. Although battle losses were by no means over (fifty-seven Tiresians fought in the American Wars of 1756–63 and only twelve returned) the Napoleonic Wars actually increased population; men with families were exempted from militia service, and island boys were marrying at sixteen.

Emigration may have been balanced for a time by immigration. There were 'not 40 natives of any other Parish' in Coll and Tiree in the 1790s, but by the 1820s the Mac-Kinnons, who probably came from clearances on Skye, outnumbered the indigenous Macleans on Rum. The terms of trade favoured the islands during the later decades of the eighteenth century, for the price of their cattle exports quadrupled but that of oatmeal (an important import to Small Isles) only doubled. Finally, seaweed gathering, which flourished early in the nineteenth century, needed much unskilled labour.

A START ON TIREE

To trace the origins of the first attempt at 'Improvement' it is necessary to go back to the early part of the eighteenth century. Unrest during and after the '15 had caused the 2nd Duke of Argyll to plant Tiree with substantial Campbell tacksmen—more to keep the peace than as agricultural innovators. They drew most of their rent in kind and labour —and a hostile people found innumerable ways of reducing it—but paid the Duke in cash; when cattle prices fell in the 1720s and 1730s many got into arrears. The 3rd Duke, a pillar of the London–Scottish Establishment which arose from the 1707 Union, needed an increasing income to keep up an increasingly grand position. Ignoring the views of his factor,

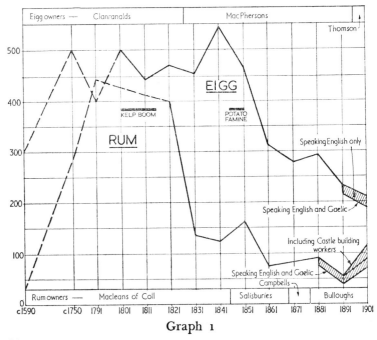

**Graph 1**

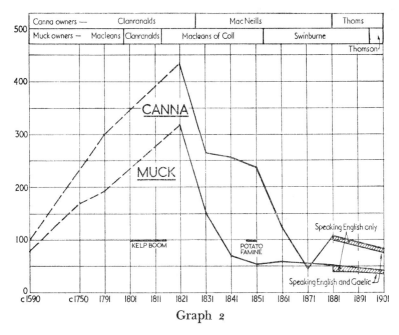

| Canna owners — | | Clanranalds | | MacNeills | | Thoms | |
| Muck owners — | Macleans | Clanranalds | Macleans of Coll | | Swinburne | | |

Graph 2

who felt that Tiree should pay *less* rent, he called in Duncan Forbes of Culloden. In August 1737 Culloden sailed for Tiree with a group of Campbell gentry, 'some gallons of whiskey' and 168 bottles of wine. His policy was simple. The tacksmen had become oppressive parasites and would be eliminated. The thirty-six farms would be re-let for cash rents paid direct to the Duke who 'had beneficent intentions of freeing the people [from] . . . oppression . . . and of giving them 19 years by lease'. Twenty-five farms were let entire, ten were divided, Ballevulin went to waste, and the rent-roll increased by £100. His Grace was delighted. 'When you have time, my curiosity makes me wish to know your observations of Teree. I have strange notions of that island.'

Culloden's policy failed. The need for quick returns led to bad farming and sandblow, and much rent remained unpaid. Several small tenants of the divided farms went bankrupt, perhaps because elimination of their tacksmen removed their only local source of credit. In the absence of the tacksmen's

69

discipline, squatting became widespread—an origin of the cottar problem of the nineteenth century. The successors to the bankrupt small tenants had no written leases—an early example of the insecurity which was to afflict island agriculture until 1886.

### INTERLUDE WITH JOHNSON AND BOSWELL

In 1773 Johnson and Boswell saw more sensible improvement attempted on Coll. When on Skye they met Donald, eldest son of Hugh Maclean of Coll, on whose advice they decided to visit Eigg ('a Popish island'), Muck, Coll and Tiree; but storms caused that ambitious programme to be abandoned.

On 3 October they left Skye for Iona. Donald told the Massacre Story as they passed Eigg on a rising sea; by nightfall a full gale caused them to make for Coll. They landed safely at Loch Eatharna on a drenching Monday morning, and avoiding the 'little poor public house close upon the

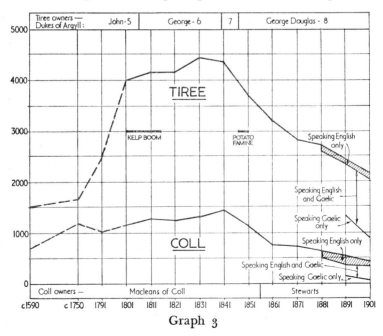

**Graph 3**

13 Ferries: *(above)* the Muck launch that meets the mailboat comes into Eigg pier *(John Currie)*;
14 *(below)* arrival at Eigg pier. The columnar basalt of Castle Island can be seen across the Sound *(John Currie)*

15 Transport: *(above)* prefabricated house for Canna arrives via Western Ferries *(Western Ferries)*;
16 *(below)* the MacBrayne steamer, *Lochearn*, was the Coll and Tiree mailboat, 1930–1955 *(Caledonian-MacBrayne)*

shore' trudged through a 'prodigious rain' to Captain Lachlan Maclean's, a mile and a half towards Arnabost. The captain, retired from the Bengal service, was building Gallanach and lived temporarily in a hut 'of stone without mortar and . . . no plastering or finishing at all. It was cold as a stable . . . the earthen floor was damp . . . There was a blazing peat fire and Mrs Maclean got us tea . . . There were some books on the board that served as a chimney piece.' The remains of the cottage, which was occupied into this century, may still be seen at the roadside. Boswell had to sleep with Donald and feared 'scorbutic symptoms' but 'upon inspection, as much as could be without his observing it, he seemed quite clean and the bed was very broad. So I lay down peaceably.'

Next morning they called on the minister, who had no church, and rode to Grishipoll an 'excellent slated house' built twenty years before (now in sad and dangerous decay) where tacksman MacSweyn and his wife gave them dinner. She wore tartan, had never been to the mainland, spoke no English and could not write, but her roast goose was delicious. They galloped on the Machair Moor, paused at the Tellers of Tales ('a Druidical temple') and finally arrived at Breachacha New Castle, a 'neat gentleman's house'. Built by the loyal Hector in 1750, it lacked its present top storey and fancy pepperpots. Most of the furniture had been removed to Aberdeen where Hugh was 'superintending' his younger children's education, and there was no 'little house'; but they were comfortable enough.

The last of the Coll's hereditary pipers, 'a decent comely fellow with a green cloth waistcoat with silver lace' played during dinner. Books were sent from the minister's library. There were family papers ('confusedly kept') to inspect and the old castle to explore. There were excursions on horseback to the 'good airing strands' of Crossapol and Feall, and to the western sandhill country, where their horses trotted 'down apparent precipices without danger, the sand always sliding away from their feet'. Maclean of Cornaig came to dine—he was the Duke's tenant for the north end of Coll and paid an 'advanced rent' to keep out Cambells. Other guests were Maclean of Crossapol and his son Donald, a Master of Arts and future minister of Small Isles, who ran Coll's only educational establishment, a vacation school. 'We were jovial tonight. Cornaig sang Erse songs. We had . . . whiskey punch . . . I came to like it well enough. I sat till after three and left them to finish a new bowl.'

Donald Maclean of Coll had studied farming in Hertfordshire (travelling down perhaps with the drovers whose route is marked by the Highlander Inn at Hitchin) and was brimful of bright ideas. He planted the first turnip-field in the Hebrides for winter keep, and 'hoed all with his own hand'. He established an orchard and planned a windbreak for it. He encouraged gardening. He started a road from Breachacha to Loch Eatharna; anticipating its completion, he imported a smith to shoe horses and carpenters to make wheeled carts. Coll even had a shop, where Boswell bought paper for his diary.

On 9 October the travellers chartered a kelp-sloop for Mull, but gales repeatedly delayed its departure and disenchantment set in; Breachacha became 'a mere tradesman's box'. They moved to Captain Maclean's house to be near the harbour, but his Highland welcome was blunted by worry about his wife's imminent confinement. Miserably, in pouring rain, they shifted to MacSweyn's. A wild night by the Grishipoll shore 'saw Mr Johnson with his handkerchief tied on his head, bringing peats'. Boswell fared better: 'Mary MacDonald, a comely black girl . . . washed my feet with warm water, which was Asiatic enough . . . I lay in clean sheets on a bed of straw.' They got away on 14 October.

Donald was drowned off Ulva in the following autumn, and his bright ideas died with him.

## ANOTHER TRY ON TIREE

On their way south Johnson and Boswell called on John, 5th Duke of Argyll ('Colonel Jack' of the '45 Militia), at

Inveraray for his factors' autumn briefing. The family estates had now reached their greatest extent (in rental terms Tiree represented a twelfth), but grandiose projects like Inveraray New Town demanded increasing revenue and Maclean of Cornaig's 'advanced rent' showed the way things were going.

In 1770 half Tiree was held by fourteen large farmers who had drained land, made hay and exported barrelled salt beef, thus avoiding the low prices commonly got for Tiree cattle, which suffered from 'bloody urine'—now known to be caused by a cobalt deficiency in machair grass. The rest was let to forty-five groups of tenants on co-operative Joint Farms, agricultural organisations probably dating from clan times. Field-strips were allocated by annual ballot. Sowing and harvesting dates were decided communally. Many horses and several men were needed for old-fashioned heavy ploughs. Cereals generally gave a pathetic three-fold return. Barley was cropped by pulling, which could cause sandblow. Winter keep was unknown; after harvest the beasts ranged the whole farm. Although labour-intensive and inefficient to the present way of thinking, joint-farming cannot have been wholly unsuccessful for in 1764 Tiresians were reported 'well-clothed and well fed, having abundance of corn and cattle'.

The main item in the Duke's Improvement was the division of Joint Farms into individual holdings to be let on nineteen-year leases (the standard holding would be rather larger than the average modern Tiree croft). It never got off the ground; few tenants could afford to stock such large holdings, which the people knew must mean redundancy. Perhaps eighty holdings could be got from the Joint Farms. Even supposing that each could support a dozen people, the total number supported would be under 1,000. Tiree's population in 1776 was around 2,100 and employment on the large farms would account for under half the deficiency.

The Duke won out on individual holdings, at the price of drastic fragmentation. In 1779 he accepted his factor's view that 'small tenants' would pay more rent. In 1803, after the Passenger Vessels Act had made emigration safer but more

costly 'the difficulty of emigration . . . makes it necessary to
. . . change my plans . . . *farms* must be broken down into
small crofts'. When he died in 1806 five-sixths of Tiree was
given over to crofters and cottars without written leases.

Other Improvements failed. Sandblow was to be reduced;
in 1804 the factor was complaining of blow caused by
ploughing machair and rooting-up barley. The Duke offered
premiums for building stone walls to eliminate herding and
crop-watching; the factor reported 'not much done'. He gave
premiums for new crops ('a few signified their wish for grass-
seed') and rotation sowing ('rotations . . . have met with little
attention'). He formed a company to exploit Balephetrish
marble and built a 12ft road to Scarinish; the quarry only
operated in 1791–4—and briefly around 1910. He encouraged
fishing; in 1804 only two boats were operating successfully.
Flax-growing for his Dunoon linen factory petered out—
there are remnants of a flaxmill at Cornaigmore.

Yet he had some success. He cut down the swarming horses
and introduced light ploughs. Cornaigmore watermill (re-
equipped about 1860) and a windmill at Scarinish were built
around 1804. Scarinish pier was built. The crisis caused by
the stripping of Tiree's sparse peat was alleviated by access to
his mosses on Mull and Coll—albeit both involved dangerous
and time-consuming journeys. He temporarily abolished
private whisky-distilling which used much peat and barley
and was illegal from the turn of the century—but only after
evictions and prosecutions, for whisky had been a valuable
export, backed by a healthy home trade. And he increased the
Tiree rent-roll from £850 to £2,500.

'IMPROVEMENT' ON OTHER ISLANDS

Donald's brother Alexander 15th of Coll who inherited in
1786 kept his problems within bounds by holding Coll's
population down (graph 3); as the only resident proprietor
on the six islands he was able to enforce a rule that any
Collach marrying without consent must leave. He limited

sandblow and improved his cattle by cutting the people's sheep from several thousand to five hundred. Around 1814 he allowed cottars to build Arinagour village, and divided land into crofts for them. He encouraged commercial fishing by importing Shetlanders, but gave a disenchanted answer when approached by the British Fisheries Society: 'If the inhabitants . . . can procure the bare necessities of life . . . from the ground . . . their ambition leads them to no further effort.'

In 1789 John MacDonald of Clanranald reserved land at Galmisdale, Eigg, for 'the Towns and Villages presently proposed for Encouragement of the fisheries', but they were never built. Two years before, he offered land around Canna harbour 'convenient for a [fishing] town', but the best site was already leased to one Hector MacNeill (a Kintyre mechant who came to Canna around 1780) who demanded £400 for not being allowed to evict its occupants. When the British Fisheries Society asked for more land 'without which we could not make the poor people perfectly independent' Clanranald demanded a prohibitive price and, despite pleas from those about to be evicted, the society's inspector accepted defeat: 'Farewell bonny Cannay the best fishery station in the Hebrides and the most tempting spot for settlement—farewell poor inhabitants.'

In 1770 Clanranald let Laig to Ranald MacDonald, son of the '45 bard, and in 1789 the rest of Eigg went to seven farmers who imported Blackface sheep ('they seem to multiply and thrive'), built march dykes and undertook to have their corn ground at 'the Mill of Eigg'; 176 people left and joint-farming was greatly reduced—although it lingered on for ninety years.

(In 1763 the Eigg mill was on Sandavaig Burn. By 1806 a leat led Sandavaig's water to a pond and mill at Kildonnan. Five years later there was insufficient water to turn the machinery and an abortive 1845 scheme proposed to capture flows from Loch nam Ban Mora; yet corn came to Kildonnan from Muck and Arisaig and around 1875 new overshot machinery was installed. The mill ceased to operate early this century.)

KELP

In 1779 the 5th Duke was already drawing the proceeds from 250 tons of kelp made annually on Tiree.

Rising populations and standards of life in the south had increased the demand for soda ash, used in manufacturing soap and glass. It could be made by burning seaweed; there are the remains of a small kelp kiln made of seashore pebbles at Balephuil Beach, Tiree. Twenty tons of weed made a ton of ash for which kelpers got £2, and shipment south might cost the same again. When the Napoleonic wars cut off rival sources and increased demand—soda ash was used in explosives—prices rose, averaging £10 between 1800 and 1820 and reaching £20 in 1810. Landlords made huge profits: Reginald George MacDonald of Clanranald netted £42,000 from kelp in 1808–10. Kelping spread to all the islands except Rum, which had little shore. Muck and Canna were virtually given over to it and the dizzy peaks of their population graphs show how labour-intensive the 'industry' was. Immigration was encouraged to keep labour-rates down. Leaders were no longer needed. Kelp drove out the tacksmen.

In 1799 the Clanranalds re-acquired Muck in payment of debts owed by Lachlan Maclean 6th of Muck (an absentee who became Governor of the Tower of London). Ten years later it was divided into forty-seven plots for kelping families, and in 1814 Alexander Maclean of Coll bought it for £9,975; he must have thought the boom would last for ever. On Eigg, Canna, Coll and Tiree many small tenants who had found their rents from cattle now found them from seaweed. Cereals declined; potatoes left more time for the shore. When the ending of the wars cut demand and allowed the import of cheaper chemicals to be resumed the trade collapsed. The islands were left packed with unemployed who contrived to exist by planting every scrap of usable ground with potatoes. They had nothing to sell and could pay no rent. By the 1820s

97 per cent of the six islands' people were classified as 'poor'.

## LANDLORDS AND PEOPLE

For this state of affairs the landlords, who had near-absolute power, were largely responsible. Young Donald Maclean told Boswell he intended to 'improve . . . without hurting the people or losing their ancient Highland fashions'; only he seems to have realised that the Improving Ideal would need to be adapted to island traditions of co-operative work on Joint Farms. His early death was a tragedy for all Gaeldom.

For the thrusting self-advancement so admired by successive Dukes of Argyll was not the Gaelic way, and inability to understand that lay at the heart of their unhappy relations with the people of Tiree. Although they were also handicapped by excessive grandeur and their incomprehensible failure to set foot on the island (the first ducal visit was in 1840), they met active obstruction only when they threatened joint-farming. When the 5th Duke tried in 1771 there was 'disaffection to the family of Argyll'; when he promoted individual crofts in 1803 there was 'growing unrest and opposition'. A different story was put about by the 8th Duke many years later: Tiree folk had always wanted crofts, and all progressive steps (there and elsewhere) had been taken 'by the proprietor'.

In the 1820s the six islands cherished three such proprietorial paragons whose 'progressive steps' were about to despatch most of their people to Glasgow and other ends of the earth. The owner of Tiree was George, 6th Duke. The owner of Eigg and Canna was Reginald George, 20th Captain of Clanranald. These absentee Etonian comics had more in common than the name George—although that was not without its significance. Both were cronies of the Prince Regent, rakes and spendthrifts who sold their lands to stave off their creditors; Reginald George ('more fitted for the soft retirement of an Asiatic harem than for the rough country to which he belongs') managed to get through the entire Clanranald estate. Alexander Maclean, proprietor of Coll, Rum and

Muck, was a very different animal, but his speculative purchase of Muck and the expensive tastes of his numerous children caused him to make the most drastic clearances in the islands' history.

A glance at the people may be refreshing. They were small: the death in 1793 of a 'country man . . . about 5 feet 10 inches high' was thought worthy of report by Tiree's parish minister. Strength was admired—and still is: the visitor may care to try Coll's 'Lifting Stones' at the roadside beyond Torostan. Primitive customs survived. The Michaelmas Cavalcade recorded on Coll and Tiree in 1703 was still observed on Canna seventy years later:

> every man . . . mounts his horse unfurnished with saddle, and takes behind him either some young girl, or his neighbour's wife, and then rides backwards and forwards from the village to a certain cross . . . After the procession . . . they alight at some public-house where, strange to say, the females treat the companions of their ride . . . An entertainment is prepared with primeval simplicity . . . a great oatcake called Struan Michael . . . composed of two pecks of meal . . . daubed over with milk and eggs . . .

The people were immensely hospitable. In 1797 Edward Daniel Clarke, a young Cambridge geologist landing at Guirdil, Rum, was 'regaled with new milk oatcakes and Lisbon wine, the freight of a wreck'. After geologising at Bloodstone he dined again on 'a clean but homely cloth . . . spread upon a board between two beds which served us for chairs, upon which was placed a collation of cream, eggs, new-milk, cheese, oatcakes and several bottles of fine old Lisbon wine'. In 1812 the geologist Necker de Saussure found the Rum folk 'the happiest in the Hebrides'. McCulloch, another geologist, was 'devoured with kindness' and played a Rum fiddle whilst his boat's crew danced reels with the barefoot island lasses. 'Where shall I go into such a house in England, find such manners and such conversation . . . and see such smoky shelves covered not only with the books of the ancients, but of the moderns . . . well thumbed and well talked of?'

In the 1790s the people of Coll and Tiree were 'cheerful and humorous' and entertained themselves 'by composing and singing songs, by repeating Fingalian and other tales [and] by dancing assemblies at different farms by turns'. The 'Fingalian tales' were remnants of a once-rich Gaelic culture. In 1776 Ranald MacDonald of Laig, son of the '45 Bard, published a book of Gaelic poems selected from his father's manuscripts. De Saussure saw them in 1812 when he visited Laig—'written in peculiar characters, long since out of use' —and drew a delightful picture of Ranald's son, Angus:

> he detained us to dinner, but before the cloth was laid, he made us drink a full glass of whiskey to the health of each . . . When the old man mentioned the Campbells, we discovered . . . some traces of animosity. But . . . all the peers of the kingdom were nothing by the side of Clanranald, his chief . . . He diverted us greatly by singing some Gaelic songs; and . . . then sung some pibrochs . . . pleasingly imitating with his voice the sound of the bagpipe . . . On our departure, the good old Laig accompanied us to the door . . . Filling a glass with whiskey, he first drank himself, and then pouring out a bumper to each in succession, we emptied it . . . a very ancient custom denominated . . . *Deoch an Dorus.*

(Angus's loyalty is touching but Clanranald's brother was of the party.) 'Nothing was more singular,' wrote de Saussure 'than his whole deportment; it was the tone, the manners of an epoch . . . long passed away.' Gaelic folk were becoming quaint.

The people's traditional dress had already gone. Small Isles parish minister in 1792:

> The men . . . wear hats, short jackets, and long trousers, instead of bonnets, short coats, and philabegs [kilts] . . . The kerchief, formerly worn by married women, and the tonnac, or short plaid, worn by females in general, are . . . out of use . . . The men . . . find the change in their dress highly convenient . . . The periodical migration of our young women to the low country in harvest, is entirely with a view to dress . . . they are a means of encouraging an extravagance.

How pleasant to know that the island lasses could annoy their staid minister! Twenty years before, when a young teacher on Coll, the Reverend Donald Maclean had beaten Boswell at drinking whisky punch . . .

Nevertheless he was right. For fear of rack-renting and eviction many islanders (not just their daughters) spent on 'extravagance' what they would have preferred to spend on improving their houses or land. Annual tenancy—imposed by landlords—was the curse of the islands until government intervened in 1886.

# 7          DISPERSAL

THE kelp slump hit Alexander Maclean very hard. When cattle prices fell after the Napoleonic wars and his Rum tenants could no longer pay their £300 rental he leased Rum to Dr Lachlan Maclean of Gallanach, Coll, for £800—as a sheepwalk. Existing arable and grazing would be needed for maximum stocking, so he got quotations for shipping 300 Rum folk to Nova Scotia. The lowest was £5.14s a head, which should quickly be recouped from Dr Lachlan's rent. The islanders received a year's notice on Whitsunday 1825.

On 11 July 1826 two ships sailed from Loch Scresort for Ship Harbour, Cape Breton. Half a century later a shepherd still recalled 'the wild outcries of the men and the heart-breaking wails of the women and children [that] filled all the air between the mountainous shores'. *St Lawrence* carried 208 people. After a fast passage of thirty-seven days they disembarked at Ship Harbour—now the oil terminal Port Hawkesbury. The local Land Commission gave each family 150 acres of bear-haunted forest (some bought more). They had seven weeks' unused rations, but autumn was approaching in a land where the mean daily minimum temperature in February shows 15° of frost. Some would find temporary homes with Rum folk who had emigrated four years before; some may even have been sheltered by the Mic-Mac Indians, whose land they were appropriating, but for most it must have been a desperate winter. (Free grants of land ceased in 1827, but people from the six islands continued to pour into Cape Breton. Some flourished, and their descendants may still be traced among the strong Gaelic community. Some went into local coalmines. Many emigrated again to the United States, and their hard-won land reverted to wilderness.)

Rum's population was reduced to fifty, of whom only one family were native, but a later influx raised it to 134 in 1831. Dr Lachlan imported a manager and 'spared neither pains nor expense' in building Kinloch House (a fragment forms part of the present post office) and in planting trees around it. But his 8,000 sheep were not as profitable as had been hoped, for the price of mutton was depressed. The doctor himself emigrated to Australia in 1839, but returned later to practise medicine in Tobermory. In the 1840s people cleared from Skye settled on the south of Scresort where they fished and kept cattle in walled enclosures; elsewhere the old villages in the lonely valleys crumbled into rising bracken.

In 1845 Alexander's son, Hugh, sold Rum to the 2nd Marquess of Salisbury for £26,455; it was the first of the six islands to pass from Scottish hands. Salisbury stocked the hill with deer and the burns with fish, and five years later conveyed the island to his son, Viscount Cranbourne, who in 1857 made another clearance, when the last native family left for Upper Canada. The ancestry of its head, Hector Maclean, is a measure of the historical continuity now ended. Hector's great-great-grandfather, Allan, settled at Kilmory. Allan's grandfather Donald was tenant of Gunna. Donald's grandfather was the 5th Maclean of Coll who sang his way out of Duart captivity in 1537. Thirteen generations connected Hector Maclean with John Garbh 1st of Coll, saved by the Gille Riabhach at the Battle of Grishipoll Burn, and twenty with Lachlan Mac-Gillean, master of ceremonies at the Eigg investiture of 1386.

In 1865 Rum passed to Cranbourne's brother, the Conservative prime minister, who let it for 10,000 sheep. Four years later it was bought by Campbell of Aros. After brief periods under Campbell of Ormsary and Campbell of Ballinaby it was auctioned in 1888 to John Bullough, textile machinery manufacturer of Oswaldtwistle.

## MUCK

In 1828 Alexander Maclean evicted 150 kelping folk from Muck—perhaps for cattle (in the 1820s and 1830s the island was leased to 'Corrychoile', the famous Lochaber drover). Some folk went to Cape Breton, but many were temporarily herded into an area above Port Mor where they extended the village of Kile. They were gone by 1841 when the population dropped to sixty-eight, and foxgloves now grow from the pathetic ruins of their short-lived cabins.

In 1854 Hugh Maclean sold Muck to Captain Thomas Swinburne RN, of Eilean Shona, Loch Moidart. He built Gallanach round a croft house and developed fishing with 20ft boats ('sufficient for Eigg Sound'), later with brown-sailed 50-footers which fished Rockall Bank; the old house at Port Mor pier was his salt-store. Swinburne let the farming to Border people who brought in Cheviots.

## CANNA

Hector MacNeill (see p 77) was succeeded by his son, Donald, who in 1820 leased the whole of Canna and bundled thirty-two families over to Sanday, still run by Clanranald Trustees. Seven years later their factor reported

> the Tenants of the Sand Island of Canna are even in a worse state than those of Cliadel on Eig, their arrears are beyond anything they can ever hope to pay . . . their residence . . . is a serious bar in the way of . . . a sale . . . the Trustees would ultimately benefit the Estate by . . . assisting them to emigrate.

No such step was needed. Canna and Sanday were sold to MacNeill who got rid of 200 people and 'built huts . . . He is very strict in his rules as to not allowing more than one family . . . in one house, and he allows no squatting . . . particularly he would not allow a public-house.' He died in 1848 at the age of seventy-nine, leaving three illegitimate children of whom Donald, the eldest, was a minor. His 'curators' let Canna to John Maclean of Glenforslan Moidart (later of Kildonnan Eigg) on condition that he cleared Kiel, the principal village, and built walls to divide the arable from the hill. Stone for the walls came from abandoned houses and St Columba's chapel—only a damaged cross now marks its site. A Tobermory contractor supervised the work; the wages paid were $1\frac{1}{2}$ stones of meal a week from potato famine relief funds. Between 1851 and 1861 Canna's population fell from 240 to 125.

Young Donald married Maclean's daughter and their children were Gaelic-speaking Catholics; but he developed expensive tastes, sending his boys to Stoneyhurst and building the present Canna House (reputedly designed by his sister Jean). He became a gross and corpulent man—it is said he was moved around in a wheelbarrow—who owed money even to his servants, for whom he divided Sunday into ten crofts. And he continued to clear. By 1871 Canna's population was down to forty-eight. According to tradition, an old woman evicted and about to go exclaimed, 'the day will come when you will leave Canna as poor as ourselves!' In 1881 debt forced MacNeill to sell the island for £23,000 to Robert Thom, a Glasgow shipowner.

## EIGG

When the Clanranald estate was dispersed, Eigg went in 1827 for £15,000 to Dr Hugh MacPherson, sometime naval surgeon, sometime Professor of Hebrew at Aberdeen, and at that time Professor of Greek. His income was under £500 and he probably received help from his uncle, Sir John MacPherson, wealthy member of the Bengal Presidency Council and former secretary to the Nawab of the Carnatic. Hugh had visited Eigg from Sleat, where his grandfather was parish minister, 'and had come to love and admire it immensely'. He adapted a pair of cottages above the harbour into Nead na Feannaig (Crow's Nest), the first Lodge. He gave long leases to the farmers at Kildonnan, Howlin and Laig, but they 'resisted all proposals for the adoption of an improved system of husbandry'. Around 1853 the MacDonalds left Laig for the USA and their land, which extended to the south coast, went to Stephen Stewart, a Border farmer, who cleared fifteen families from the Grulins—'So sweet were the grasses which grew there that all his ewes had twins.' Most of the Grulin folk went across the Atlantic, but Finlay MacCormick got a croft at Cleadale where his grandson, Hugh MacKinnon, one of the greatest tradition-bearers in Eigg's history, died in 1972. Brae was cleared in 1858 to build Kildonnan fank (sheep fold). Sandavaig (behind the Manse) and Tolain, near Howlin, went rather later.

When Hugh MacPherson died in 1854 the island passed to some of his numerous children, notably Norman, Professor of Scots Law at Glasgow, and Isabella, who lived at Nead na Feannaig for half a century, a Lady Bountiful and uncrowned queen of the island. Much woodland was planted, the lochs were stocked with trout and black-houses were gradually replaced; few remained by 1881. During the 1870s Eigg enjoyed a modest prosperity, mostly from wool and commercial potato-growing. The population actually increased; as one of Isabella's sisters wrote: 'no one will move, they all adore the place'.

### COLL

In 1815 George, the 6th Duke, sold Cornaig and Caoles, the ends of Coll, for £8,000 to the sitting tenants, Malcolm and Murdoch Campbell, sons of the tacksman of Torostan. Alexander Maclean, promised first refusal, 'was disappointed'. Perhaps he lacked cash; he was currently paying £9,975 for Muck in three annual instalments. He retired in 1828, died in 1835, and is buried in Maclean's tomb at the east end of Crossapol Bay. His enterprising guardee son, Hugh, built a mansion at Tobermory 'at the expense of settlers under the British Fisheries Society' and introduced pig farming to Coll —500 animals were exported in 1839. Captain Donald

Campbell appeared as factor, cleared Gallanach for sheep despite warnings about sandblow, and drained land behind the coastal dunes. He was a redoubtable evicter; the 1841 Census lists twenty-six persons 'in barns' and fifty 'absent in search of employment', and he later cleared Feall and Torostan. Four centuries of Maclean ownership came to an end in 1856 when Hugh Maclean sold Coll estate to John Lorne Stewart, chamberlain to the Duke of Argyll.

### THE LAST FAMINE

In 1846 potatoes failed all over the West Highlands and government sent an 'experienced Commissariat Officer' north. Despite an ominous name Sir Edmund Coffin, who served in Irish famine relief, was ideally suited to the task of supervising such help as the *laisser-faire* views of the time allowed. The navy brought Indian corn to Tobermory to be sold at pre-famine prices. Under Scottish poor law no 'able-bodied' person could be relieved, and Sir Edmund had to persuade landlords to buy food for their people or to find them paid work—usually on drainage, for which loans were available. Much money was given by national famine relief organisations.

On his way north Sir Edmund conferred with the ailing 7th Duke, who urged emigration, and his chamberlain, who talked of the 'obstinately indolent habits of the people'. After several abortive attempts a party from HMS *Firefly* managed to land on Tiree in October. There was only three weeks' food and the starving people were living on shellfish and seed-corn. In that winter of bitter gales the next news of Tiree came just before Christmas when an island smack put into Tobermory: the Duke had sent 400 bolls of meal (about 10lb per head), but the store had been robbed, the people lacked fuel and some had died of typhus and cholera. The parish minister asked for 15 tons of food and would pay cash on delivery—from Free Church funds.

Meanwhile the Marquis of Lorne, the Duke's son and heir,

88

17 Old Breachacha Castle, Coll, still inhabited;

18 Celtic Christianity. The Old Cross, Canna, on the site of St Columba's chapel *(Violet Banks)*

19 *(above)* 'Clanranald's prison', Canna. Sanday and Bloodstone Hill, Rum, in the distance *(Violet Banks)*;

20 *(below)* Viking ship burial remains at Rubha Langan-Innis, Canna. The hills of South Uist across the Sea of the Hebrides *(Violet Banks)*

corresponded with the Home Secretary: 'Whatever may be
. . . the duty of landlords, it is difficult to conceive it as
extending beyond the income derived from their estates.' He
got a robust reply: 'Tiree was only a small part of [his
father's] estates, and bad years must be taken with good.'
Told that Sir Edmund was unhappy with the factor's reports,
Lorne bridled and got an apology. When forty Tiree men
'for whom we had actually procured work near Glasgow' left
it because they were paid only 9 shillings a week, he was
outraged; half the population ought to be sent to Canada.
Whilst Sir Edmund's officers risked their lives to land on
Tiree, Lorne wrote successively from Inveraray, Castle
Howard, Trentham and Bournemouth, soliciting money to
get rid of his father's people.

In January 1847 Colonel Jack Campbell (the 'Black
Factor') returned to Tiree having been absent since early
October. Later that month 135 'heads of families' started
drainage work after a brave and bitter struggle over the
starvation wages he offered. In May eighty men went south,
under a Free Church scheme, to build railways and 300
people left for Cape Breton, assisted by the Duke.

As early as September Hugh Maclean bought Indian meal
in Glasgow. He borrowed £2,000 for enclosure and drainage
—'I hear of pipe tiles in Ayrshire and am inquiring'—and
with other proprietors got a £5,000 loan for roadworks—'all
the surveys . . . have been made long ago'. He got Mr Hume,
currently building Ardnamurchan Lighthouse, to survey a
pier site at Arinagour, collected sound potatoes for seed and
supported thirty-five island families when their men went
south to find work.

When Sir Edmund sent *Shearwater* to Eigg in January,
Dr MacPherson, a sick man, had not been seen on the island
since 1841; his son Norman had been over and 'talked a great
deal but did nothing', and the factor was in eastern Scotland.
The minister was already draining his glebe. Young Angus
MacDonald of Laig was 'thinking of emigrating' but 'might
do some draining if he stayed'. The island road lay unfinished

although the people wanted work. Two sacks of meal were left and starvation was imminent. Dr Hugh's solicitors wrote complacently: 'It was satisfactory . . . that there was a supply of food on Eigg . . . the Factor . . . had not failed to attend to the instructions . . . that supplies of meal should be . . . sold *on credit* at cost price. The Factor's expenditure had exceeded £120 and he had £50 in hand.' They went on to make Lorne's point about the limit of a landlord's liability and finished with the customary comments about the people's 'idleness and apathy'. Fortunately Free Church supplies were soon forthcoming. That summer Dr Hugh's daughter Christina wrote: 'Papa has I am sorry to say suffered at the utmost possible extent receiving no rent and feeding many hundred of people in Eigg a position you must feel . . . to be by no means a convenient one.'

# 8     TIREE AFTER THE FAMINE

WHEN Lorne became 8th Duke in 1847 he refused an offer for Tiree by 'a great agricultural improver' whom he feared 'would deal rather too summarily with the excessive population'. Was this his chamberlain, John Stewart?

In 1851 375 crofters were on annual tenancy, without leases. The tacksmen's holdings at Hough Hynish and the Reef and the minister's at Balephetrish were relatively small. £11,000 had been spent on drainage and famine relief. £3,800 rent was owing.

|  | number | population | rental |
|---|---|---|---|
| crofters (average 9 cattle) | 152 | 960 | £2,056 |
| crofters (average 2 cattle) | 223 | 1,400 | £580 |
| landless cottars | 232 | 1,458 | – |
| fishermen (say) | 15 | 95 | nil? |

Cottars earned 7 shillings a fortnight on drainage (nearly completed). When crops held up the work they fell back on shellfish and famine relief (nearing exhaustion). 825 people petitioned to go to Cape Breton, for potatoes had not been re-established and 'your Petitioners' prospects are in the extreme dismal'.

The Duke was normally engaged in parliamentary duties but in the summer of 1850 'as there was nothing to interest me in the session' he visited Tiree: 'My enjoyment was greatly enhanced by seeing the happy effects upon the people of the policy I had entered upon.' Tiree became a 'dry' island. Emigration was encouraged by partial payment of passage money, raising rents, and evicting for arrears; those sheltering the evicted were threatened with eviction themselves. Land thus made vacant was added to tacksmen's holdings (as at Hynish) or consolidated to form farms (as at Heylipoll). Farmers had leases and the right to keep sheep; crofters had neither.

In 1861 the Duke leased land at Sandaig to Edward Stanford, a chemist who had developed a process for making iodine from seaweed. He built Tiree's first factory. Boilers had to be landed across open beaches. There was no road to the site. The natives were hostile.

> Some thought [me] a Frenchman, and their ideas about Napoleon were still very warlike . . . others thought my idea was to dig up dead bodies and boil them down for fat (there was little enough of that to spare amongst the living); others, the majority, took a violent hatred against me because they thought I was an excise officer sent to look for the illicit stills.

In the end he 'got on very well', training his own bricklayers smiths and fitters—and bringing gas to local premises. He reduced the factor's estimate of available weed from 120,000 tons a year to 16,000, but less was actually gathered and the factory never prospered. Collectors received sixpence a cubic yard paid in 'lines' on the Seaweed Company's shop.

The Black Factor left in 1862. Two years later his successor Geikie carried out the last major evictions, to form Scarinish Farm. Pressure eased under John MacDiarmid appointed in 1874, but there had been radical changes. MacDiarmid held Heylipoll and Crossapoll, and four farmers had Scarinish, Balephetrish, Cornaigmore, Hough and Greenhill on nineteen-year leases at rents totalling £3,000. Labour-intensive cereals had given way to Highland and cross-Shorthorn stores, Blackface and Leicester sheep and commercial potatoes. Crofting had suffered:

|              | *1851*                      | *1881*                          |
| ------------ | --------------------------- | ------------------------------- |
| holdings     | 375                         | 196                             |
| location     | virtually all the island    | poor ground, E end and W coast  |
| rental       | £2,636                      | £2,400                          |
| average rent | £7                          | £12                             |

annual tenancy, without leases. Smallest viable holding £15

The population was 2,730. There were a few weavers, who were not allowed to keep sheep, and some fishermen, limited to 20ft boats by lack of piers. A hundred or two depended on the farms; 1,200 on crofting. Another 1,200 were cottars' families who found decreasing work on seaweed collection or, according to Stanford, 'lived on the strong air'. Such were the happy effects of thirty years of the Duke's consolidation policy.

But change was in the air. The conservative influence of the Presbyterian church was shaken by the Disruption. Scheduled steamer services started in the 1860s, and in 1881 the Oban railway brought Glasgow within a day's journey. Coal supplanted peat for all but the poorest when the Duke ceased to give access to his Mull and Coll mosses. Tea, coffee and factory-made loaves were replacing milk, porridge and barley-bread—partly due to fashion, partly to the decrease in croftland. Newspaper articles read aloud were replacing 'Fingalian tales' at the ceilidh. A Tiree branch of the Highland Land-Law Reform Association, the 'Land League', was formed; there was also one on Coll.

Poverty was sharpened by potato-blight around 1880, when the Lord Mayor of London's fund supplied seed, but Argyll estates refused other help. A high tide in 1881 flooded cottars' houses and added to general wretchedness.

On 6 August 1883 Lord Napier's Commission of Inquiry into the Conditions of Crofters and Cottars in the Highlands and Islands of Scotland sat before a packed audience in Gott church and asked 991 questions. MacDiarmid was unable to specify any 'overt act' which would demonstrate the Duke's interest in his islanders, other than books for school prizes and clothes for the poor. Alexander Buchanan, island doctor since 1860, would not reply when asked if 'a fair proportion' of rents had gone into 'benevolent and useful work'; the Duke latterly spent a day or two on Tiree each summer but 'no change' could be seen 'from his coming and going'. Some evidence was fanciful, but basic needs were clear: security of tenure, fair rents, compensation for improvements and more land.

Gladstone's Crofters Bill of 1885 was dropped when his government resigned. Disappointment caused unrest on Tiree; a gunboat was seen cruising offshore and the police force doubled from one to two. At an autumn general election (the first after Gladstone's Enfranchisement Act became operative) island men experienced the pleasing novelty of having their votes solicited. Fraser Mackintosh, a member of Napier's Commission, was returned as People's Candidate for Inverness-shire (on Eigg he found 'the priest . . . and the Free Church minister . . . in perfect sympathy with the people . . . on the Land Question'). A Crofter's Candidate captured Argyll, long held by the Duke's sons. After returning to power Gladstone brought in another Bill which despite ducal opposition received royal assent early in 1886. Under the Crofters (Scotland) Holdings Act crofters paying under £30 rent and cottars paying under £6 received compensation on outgoing for improvements they had made and access to a court to determine fair rents. Crofters received fixity of tenure. But the provisions about more land were manifestly inoperable.

Land-hungry crofters no longer feared eviction; with a Conservative government again in power and the local Crofters' Candidate defeated the stage was set for confrontation. It might never have happened on Tiree had the Duke not provided a *casus belli*, for crime was unknown, the islanders were 'quiet and peaceable', and the doctor at least 'never got an uncivil word'.

When in 1886 the lessee of Greenhill Farm emigrated to Australia the Tiree branch of the Land League led by their secretary Lachlan MacNeill, the emigrant's brother, urged the Duke to divide the farm and resolved that anyone offering to take it all would be 'hung to the chimney of the White House of Greenhill'. Lachlan himself made such an offer which the Duke accepted. In protest, seventy-five islanders drove their beasts to the Greenhill fields. The Duke issued seventy-five Notices of Interdict. The Sheriff's Officer required to serve them was given a protection-party of police and forty Glasgow Commissionaires, under the Chief Constable of Argyll.

MacBrayne's Oban agent refused to carry them and a private vessel was chartered. After difficulty in sailing (no Oban man would cast-off) and landing (no Tiresian would man the ferry) they got ashore on the afternoon of 21 July, hired a pair of carriages from Scarinish Hotel and set off towards Greenhill, looking and perhaps feeling like a funeral party in search of a coffin. The islanders were indignant at this official support for the Duke's civil action, and near Balephuil 200 people barred further progress. The Chief Constable warned them of the consequences of 'deforcing' a Sheriff's Officer but they were in no mood for reason. Noisy exchanges frightened the horses, the carriages went careering off and the party retreated on the hotel, where they spent an anxious night listening to pipers playing to a ribald crowd. Next morning they embarked for Oban where on Friday the 23rd the Commissionaires were roundly jeered as they boarded the southbound train.

That day HM troopship *Assistance* lay in Portsmouth, her crew ashore. During the afternoon an Admiralty telegram put her on two hours' notice; messengers were sent scurrying round the town but many men were left behind when she sailed. On Saturday (when *The Times* report opened 'There is war in Tiree') she put into Plymouth to embark 146 marines for Oban. Four days later HMS *Ajax* brought 100 more. Meanwhile Oban was filling with police (700 according to one report!) and the trawler *Nigel* was chartered to take them. On Friday 30 July, the three ships sailed down the Sound of Mull.

Tiree was in holiday mood. Factor MacDiarmid, alarmed by noisy crowds dancing reels before Island House, had left the island. Old men engaged in the congenial occupation of feeding rumours to gullible reporters: the blacksmith was working day and night forging spears and enormous cudgels; a hundred guns were hidden away; Dr Buchanan had ordered extra bandages. The ships entered Gott Bay at sunset. At midnight an advance party landed across sands glittering in a blaze of naval searchlights. Not a soul was to be seen. Only the murmur of family prayers through open windows broke the silence of a warm summer night.

Next morning bugles blared over sunlit water as the main force assembled for landing. They pitched tents on Scarinish machair, formed column of route and set off for the West End, each man with twenty rounds. The day was hot, the tracks were dusty, and the men were soon consumed with thirst; bowls of milk came from cottage after cottage. After twelve hours tramping the weary troops returned to Scarinish, their last miles enlivened by the marine band, summoned ashore by heliograph—a wonder and delight to the island children. As the days went by, the marines and police got on famously with the people, who found for the first time that tourism brought new life, new ideas and extra cash. The officers had a golf-course laid out, the sailors arranged tours of *Ajax* and the marines helped with the harvest. There were daily musical marches. The only trouble arose when a reporter described some respectable old ladies as 'the Witches of Kilkenneth'—an indignant son was fined at Tobermory court for breaching the peace.

The accused: George Campbell, Colin Henderson, Gilbert MacDonald, Hector MacDonald, John MacFadyen, Donald

MacKinnon, Alexander Maclean and John Sinclair agreed to 'come quietly'. At midnight on Friday 6 August they sailed for Inveraray, each carrying a bible. Released on bail, they were led to the pier by a piper and cheered within sight and sound of the Duke's castle. A whip-round was organised on *Lord of the Isles* en route to Glasgow where they were the star turn at a public meeting. On 18–20 October they appeared before Lord Mure in Edinburgh and after a trial of doubtful fairness a unanimous jury found them guilty of mobbing, rioting and deforcement, 'with a strong recommendation to leniency'. Mure sentenced five to six months and the rest to four, 'the most lenient sentences ever pronounced', or so he said.

Protest meetings were held throughout Scotland and petitions poured in. Tiree women wrote to the Queen:

> . . . the men are all of good character and did not know that shouting at law officials is a grave offence. We are all so peaceful on Tiree that policemen hardly ever come near us. We have had many years of poverty . . . Our forefathers defended your Majesty's throne and our husbands and sons and brothers would do so again. We are all poor women and cannot see our Queen but we know she has a mother's heart and will give ear to our humble petition. It is the year of your Majesty's Jubilee and we pray you make it ever memorable to us by setting the captives free.

Only one-third could sign their names. The men also petitioned:

> The prisoners who simply protested against the present state of the Land Laws without being guilty of violence towards anyone, have been refused the right of trial by their equals, for Edinburgh men are not like the people of the Western Isles in their ways . . .

The Home Secretary, fearing demonstrations, ordered the Tiree Martyrs to be released. On 26 January 1887 they were smuggled on to *Dunara Castle* at Greenock and sailed for home. All was quiet on the island. The marines and police had gone, and were greatly missed. For decades to come

Tiresians would tell their children of the soldiers, the search-lights, the heliograph and the band; above all they liked to recall the sports day when an island team beat all comers at tug-o'-war. Half a century later the author of the first Tiree guidebook would write 'boys that saw the Soldiers Sports of 1886 on Scarinish machair will not forget them till their dying day—a spectacle of awe and wonder'. Not until the 1940s, when the lively lads of the RAF came swarming in, did the island know such times again.

### AFTERMATH

The Duke never again set foot on Tiree. Yet the next two decades saw a member of his family resident; despite paternal discouragement his daughter, Lady Victoria Campbell, crippled victim of polio, stayed with the MacDiarmids at Island House in September 1886 (when the Martyrs were awaiting trial), wintered at Balemartine in 1891–3 and—of all places—at Greenhill in 1893–4. Around 1897 a house at Gott, formerly a school, was enlarged for her and became the Lodge (now the Lodge Hotel). This brave busybody established a YWCA, bible, sewing and woodwork classes, and soup-kitchens ('tremendous morning of Soup Crusade'), persuaded her father to subsidise dairy cows so that cottars' children might have milk, and arranged for the first district nurse. Lady Victoria lived intermittently on the island until 1909 and died in Rome in 1910. Her simple memorials are the pulpit in Heylipoll church, carved by a member of her woodwork class, and a plaque in Kirkapoll church.

The colourful events of 1886 had no effect on landholding. The large farms, including Greenhill, remained intact for twenty-five years. By 1894, when much farm land was 'over-grown . . . with rushes and rough grass', the 196 crofters of 1881 had decreased to 184, and 200 cottars had increased to 250. Argyll County Council received numerous applications for smallholdings, but as granting them meant taking farmers' land nothing was done—Councillor MacDiarmid had Heylipoll,

Councillor Barr had Crossapoll Reef and Balephetrish. In 1895 a government Commission reported all farms, except Balephetrish and Scarinish, as suitable for division into crofts —pointless in the absence of compulsory powers. (Grulins, Galmisdale, Struidh and Howlin on Eigg; northern Rum from Guirdil to Kinloch, western Canna and eastern Muck were also 'suitable'.)

The 8th Duke died in 1900 and was succeeded by his son John Douglas, estranged husband of Princess Louise, sometime Governor-General of Canada ('the Highlanders . . . in Cape Breton . . . kissed my hand'). He was soon warning crofters against 'insolence', asking the Congested Districts Board for land to which they might be 'migrated' and refusing smallholdings to cottars ('you should enlist in the Naval Reserve'). In 1902 he put Tiree on the market at £130,000 and would have taken £30,000 less. Cottars repeatedly asked the County Council for 'potato land and grazing for a cow' under the new Allotment Act, but nothing was done. When they hinted they might help themselves their letter was returned. They wrote again 'hoping you will excuse us for former application' but this was not considered 'explicit withdrawal' so again, nothing was done. Even Lady Victoria thought there was 'mismanagement' on Tiree.

But the crofters, who felt secure enough to improve what land they had, earned a modest share in Edwardian agricultural prosperity. Some went into egg production, worth £2,000 a year by 1906. Some developed a trade in heavy horses. Many built new houses—disappointing to those in search of the quaint, but a great improvement on most of the old cottages. Yet, whilst landholding was so inequitable and the fires of poor kelp-gatherers lit Tiree beaches, this could not be a stable society. In 1913, 210 Tiresians applied to the Land Court for crofts. Its chairman took a refreshingly novel view, whatever one may think of his jargon: 'the islanders have inherent qualities of industry and business capacity that should ensure the further crofterisation of the island a very fair trial'. He recommended dividing Hynish,

Balephetrish, Baugh and Greenhill (old Lachlan MacNeill was to keep the farmhouse). Hynish was split into twenty-two crofts when the tenant died later that year, but little else was done before World War I, and in 1918 there were 'disturbances' at Balephetrish.

Under the 10th Duke, Balephetrish, Reef and Crossapoll were divided for ex-servicemen and the Tiree show (defunct since 1891) was revived. Crofting again spread throughout the island and by 1928 the parish clerk was able to tell a government committee, 'We are a prosperous community farming a fertile island.' Annual exports included 1,000 cattle, 4,000 sheep, 200 pigs, 40,000 dozen eggs and 1,500 cran of herrings. In 1948 Major Iain MacLennan was appointed factor; before his retirement in 1974 crofters attained an individual level of output their grandfathers would have thought impossible.

There are three principal reasons for Tiree's pre-eminence in Scottish crofting. The land is good, although not easy to farm; the Argylls contributed towards drainage, limiting sandblow, and agricultural education. The people fought for their rights; the Argylls ultimately conceded them—with a good grace. Above all, the crofts are large enough to be viable; is the 8th Duke not smiling to himself as he pursues his lofty task of consolidating the Elysian Fields?

# 9        HIMSELF—THE ISLAND
## PROPRIETOR

EIGG

ROBERT Thomson (1841–1913), bachelor son of John MacEwen of Inverness, *Times* foreign correspondent and international armaments salesman, bought Eigg, Muck and Strathaird (Sleat of Skye) in the 1890s. Some remarkable letters were produced when in 1904 he sued Armstrong-Whitworth for unpaid commission: 'I shall try to see the Mikado with regard to the model of your new battle-ship . . . I shall try to show the model to the Emperor of China . . . I intend . . . to make the increase in the American naval force very clear to the Japanese.' His money and a capable factor at Kildonnan, Andrew Glendinning, made the islands prosper—Eigg even acquired a motor-boat ferry. He took up residence at Eigg Lodge on Diamond Jubilee Day 1897. That night bonfires lit the summer dim; one on the Sgurr to honour the Queen, another below Galmisdale House for the new proprietor. His change of name and Far East connections fascinated the islanders: gold and silver swords lay in cases in his 'Curio Room'—presents for Japanese army and navy chiefs, for some reason never despatched; he took long walks, alone, by night; he dined with a place set for a visitor who never arrived . . . had he come to Eigg to escape assassins? In 1913, a sick old man sitting at a window, he watched his own grave dug at the highest point of Castle Island and on Christmas Day his body was buried there, under a polished marble slab, in the most beautiful grave-site in all the Hebrides.

The estates passed to his brother, John, and Eigg shootings were let to a Dane who bought the island in 1916. Sir William Peterson (1856–1925), a huge and irascible man, son of a grocer, was a considerable London shipowner. The old Lodge burnt down during his first year and he replaced it in 1920 by a 'Spieresque Plasmentic house of timber and plastic strengthened by perforated steel plates' (the old factor's house to the north is of similar exotic construction); the builders had to take him to court to get their money. In 1925 this second Lodge burnt down whilst Sir William was on the island. He died that year and was buried 'in a glass-sided coffin, wearing evening dress and a gold chain'.

Stability returned with the next owner, Sir Walter Runciman (1870–1949), cabinet minister in various governments from 1908, shipping and insurance magnate. Around 1930 he built the present Lodge; Balfour Paul of Edinburgh designed a beautiful harled and limewashed Italianate house and laid out its glorious subtropical gardens in the shelter of the MacPhersons' mature plantations. A public hall was placed on the old Lodge site and a doctor's house built by the gates. A warehouse and waiting-room were provided at the pier, cottages and farms were modernised, tractors introduced, and there was large-scale forestry. When the National Government was formed in 1931 Sir Walter was summoned from Eigg by radio to be President of the Board of Trade; he became a viscount when Chamberlain took over in 1937. He is chiefly remembered for his 1938 mission to mediate between the Sudeten Germans and the Czech government—a futile exercise which he took on only after the personal intervention of George VI. Suffering from Parkinson's disease, Runciman resigned office at the outbreak of war, came occasionally to Eigg for the fishing in the early war years and died in 1949.

The island passed to his sons, Walter, the 2nd Viscount, and Sir Steven, the distinguished historian. Steven wrote many books in the quiet of the Lodge ('people who telephoned never tried twice'), spoke some Gaelic ('and under-

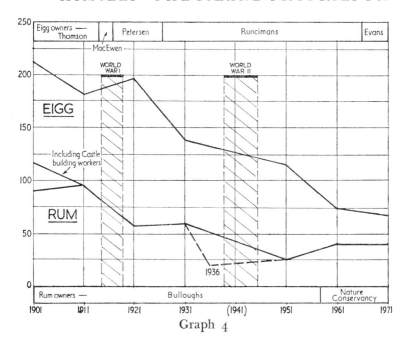

Graph 4

stood more') and was a popular if retiring figure when on the island; for twenty years he gave the children an Easter party. His friends came to stay: Princess Marina (by helicopter from Tiree), Prince Obolensky, Arthur Bliss, Lord Adrian, Noel Annan, Freya Stark, Yehudi Menuhin ('a handy man for the ceilidh tonight', as a crofter put it).

Conscious that future generations might not retain their interest, the Runcimans sold Eigg in 1966 to Robert Evans who farms extensively in the Welsh Border country. He aimed to develop farming, and was very sensitive to the fragility of his unique community; but for personal and health reasons he sold the island in 1971 to Bernard Farnham-Smith's Anglyn Trust, which ran a school for handicapped children in Sussex. They planned a similar establishment on Eigg, to develop tourism and agriculture (they had farmed their Sussex estate), and to make the community more self-sufficient by running a boat service and building a small abattoir. Their excellent intentions were, however, not realised and in 1975 Eigg was again sold. The new owner, Keith Schellenberg, director of Udny and Dudwick Estates, who owns large farms in Aberdeenshire, promptly electrified the island by landing his private plane at Kildonnan in mid-winter.

CANNA

Robert Thom (1825–1911) who bought Canna in 1881 owned sailing ships in the South American trade. He came to the island only occasionally, but his son Allan (1870–1934) lived at Tigh Ard (the High House), built in the 1890s, and was for many years Small Isles' County Councillor. The Thoms were popular proprietors who provided good cottages and encouraged gardening by annual prizes.

In 1938 Thom's widow sold the island to John Lorne Campbell of Inverneill—in Gaelic style, John son of Duncan son of Duncan son of James son of Duncan son of Sir James Campbell who with his brother (a military engineer who made a fortune in India) bought Inverneill, Loch Fyne, in 1773. With Compton Mackenzie, John Campbell founded the Sea League in 1933, to preserve the Minch for native fishermen. With Sir Alexander MacEwen he advocated a Highland Development Board thirty years before the present Highlands and Islands Development Board (HIDB). His many services to Gaelic literature and culture were recognised when in 1965 he was made D. Litt; his wife, Margaret Fay Shaw, a Pennsylvanian, published *Folk Songs and Folk Lore of South Uist*, the product of twenty years' loving labour.

Highland farming was depressed in 1938 and the agents' prospectus talked of snipe and woodcock. The population was 45; the stock was 45 Galloways, 475 Black Face and 500 Cheviots. There were 3,000 acres of good hill, $8\frac{1}{2}$ of plough, and Sanday had ten well-cultivated crofts. Mechanisation started immediately after the war. A valuable herd of pedigree highland cattle was built up, and 14 acres of beautiful mixed woodland was added to the Thoms' 5. John

21 People: *(above)* a wedding at Arinagour, Coll, 1971 *(Laird Parker)*;
22 *(below)* one of Eigg's greatest tradition-bearers, Hugh MacKinnon,
1894–1972 *(John Currie)*

23 Wildlife: *(above)* Peter Wormell, chief warden on Rum 1957–1973, with a shearwater just taken from its burrow high on Hallival *(Syndication International)*;
24 *(below)* weighing a red deer calf on Rum *(Dr B. Mitchell)*

Campbell's right-hand man for over thirty years was 'Big Hector' MacDonald, a crofter born on the island, who in 1964 received from the Queen Mother a bar to his Highland Society Long Service Medal. 'I've never taken a holiday in my life . . . when I go away it's to a cattle sale or show. I've no regrets. I've had a very complete life . . . things have got better and better—water in the houses, free electricity, good wages, a master who puts your interests before his own.' Big Hector died in 1975. John Campbell himself says: 'This is a good farm, and I would say I break about even. I'm doing what I consider to be my natural duty. I measure my success here by the happiness of the people of Canna. It is a way of life in which I happen to believe.'

### MUCK

Muck dairying prospered under Robert Thomson; there were forty milking cows and 8olb cheeses were exported. His brother John rented the island out for sheep until his death in 1922 when it passed to his son, Commander William MacEwen RN (1893–1967). The Commander brought up his family at Gallanach, planted shelter and amenity trees and ran a farm accepted as a model for island agriculture. In Fraser Darling's words, the tiny community was 'held together by a tenacious and benevolent private ownership', an achievement not easily appreciated by mainland folk. Muck's increasingly formidable challenge continues to be met with energy and resource by the Commander's son, Lawrence, as the eighth decade of the MacEwen regime approaches.

### COLL

The Stewarts are in their twelfth decade on Coll. John Lorne Stewart, whose grandfather fought at Culloden, held lands in Glenbuckie and Kintyre. When he bought Coll estate in 1856 some fanciful tales were told: 'I have been informed that when Mr Stewart collected his first rent in the parish church

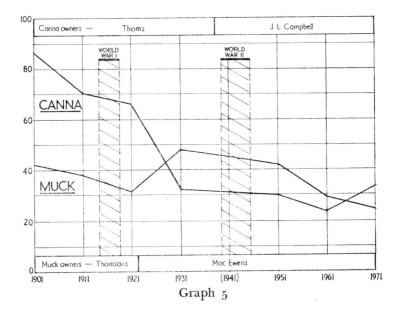

Graph 5

he exhibited a six-chambered revolver.' That 'evidence' was given by a Collach aged twenty-nine to the Commission on Crofting Land in 1894.

Stewart cleared 19 Arinagour crofts in 1857, when 81 Collachs sailed in the *Persian* for Tasmania—8 are said to have died en route; and 9 Grishipoll crofts went in the following year, when 15 families trekked north to Cornaig, owned by Neil Campbell, nephew of the Campbell brothers (see p 87)—who had made a fortune in Australia. The 1937 guide recalls this exodus: 'Infants carried in arms over back or in creels hung on the horses' pack saddles; the children . . . each with his or her own load, the cattle driven in front, a shelter for the night improvised.' In all Stewart reduced 70 crofts to 11; but he imported Kintyre dairying folk Ayrshire cattle and much capital. He built a sawmill and meal-mill at Acha, and most of the present farms. Henceforward a principal product was to be cheese, a compact and preservable export: 60 tons were exported annually. The people themselves built up fish exports (mostly ling) to 120 tons a year. Stewart's son, Colonel John, who succeeded in 1878, encountered depression when Dutch and American cheeses swamped the market, and cattle prices fell so low that in 1899 Coll calves were killed at birth.

In 1907 Colonel John was succeeded by his brother, a naval officer, and ten years later the estate passed to his grandson Charles Edward Stewart, for many years a member of Argyll County Council. In the 1920s even crofts were lying vacant, and there was reversion to stockraising. In 1932 the estate went to a second cousin, Brigadier-General Ernest Paul (1864 –1942), an engineer officer born in Australia and living in retirement in London. General Stewart—as he was henceforth known—came to live at Breachacha, adopted the kilt, advertised Kilbride Acha Totamore and Arileod to let, and brought his organisational and engineering experience to bear on Coll's problems. Despite efforts to participate in government's milk marketing scheme, dairying languished; five farms were vacant in 1937 and the Breachacha cheese

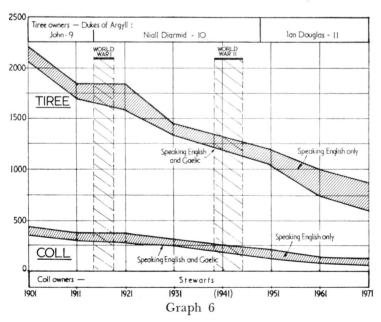

Graph 6

factory closed. The General planned a pier, vocational training, poultry-keeping, bee-keeping, 'modernising' the cottages at Arinagour and piped water for the village; in the 1930s he did well to succeed with the last two. He left Breachacha in 1941 and died in London the following year. He is buried in the modest Stewart graveyard at Arinagour and was succeeded by his son, Colonel William, who was killed in World War II; the 7th Stewart of Coll is his grandson, C. K. M. Stewart, who now lives at Acha House, formerly Acha school.

RUM

John Bullough (1838–91) rented Rum shootings from 1879 and bought the island nine years later. His father, James, was a Lancashire hand-loom weaver whose talent for invention brought him wealth. John was an inventor, a mechanical engineer and an astute manager whose abounding energy embraced shooting, racing, cock-fighting, boxing, music, poetry and Conservative politics—he was a great admirer of the Marquess of Salisbury, a predecessor on Rum. In 1868 he bought Meggernie, once Campbell of Glenlyon's, a Perthshire estate of 50sq miles. Yet when Rum came on the market he bought that too—he had contracted 'island fever', an incurable infection. He built a shooting-box at Harris and staff houses at Kinloch—'with ovens and hot-water apparatus'. Guided by the naturalist Harvie-Brown, he planted 80,000 trees around Scresort—many of which failed—and planned $\frac{1}{2}$ million more. He wintered with his family at Kinloch House in 1887–90 and his eldest son, George (1870–1939), shot his first stag in Glen Harris on Boxing Day 1888. When John died suddenly in a London hotel in 1891, George inherited Rum, the Globe textile machinery works at Accrington, and vast wealth. He was twenty-two and the world lay at his feet: he went right round it in his huge steam-yacht *Rhouma*. In 1900 he refitted her as a Boer War hospital ship and sailed to Cape Town, receiving a knighthood for his trouble.

Sir George loved Rum. His wealth enabled him to lavish that love on the island with such gusto and magnificence that for the first decade of this century it entered the realms of fantasy. In 1899 an army of workmen descended on the bemused islanders. Kinloch House was demolished. Relays of ships brought red sandstone from Arran, and Kinloch Castle arose. Gardens were laid out and glasshouses built. More staff houses went up and the last of the old cabins was abandoned. The little timber chapel/school was replaced by the substantial building still in use. Shelter-belts and land-scaped woods were planted. Roads were pushed through to Harris and Kilmory. A shooting-box was built at Papadil. Close to old John's burial place on the cliffs above Harris Bay there arose a family mausoleum in the form of an elegant Doric temple. Nor were more mundane matters neglected: at lonely and lovely Kilmory the remains may still be seen of a large, well-equipped, corrugated-iron laundry.

In the spring of 1903 Sir George brought a fairy queen to reign over his island—and, it is said, over him. Monica, daughter of the 3rd Marquess de la Pasture of Paris and London, was a dream of beauty who moved in the glittering society frequented by Edward VII. Although she was a divorcee, old John Sinclair (Small Isles' minister) married the happy pair at Kinloch Castle on 24 June, amid an exotic gathering of the aristocracy and plutocracy.

Kinloch Castle stands at the head of Loch Scresort behind wide lawns rising gently to embrace the terrace on which it is set. It is a two-storey structure about 150ft square—traditionally the length of *Rhouma*—built round a central courtyard. There are squat turrets at each corner. A turreted tower culminates in a high platform where a piper played at sunset. A glass-roofed colonnade runs round the house. All is duly castellated.

It is over sixty years since the castle was fully occupied, yet its furnishings remain intact. A modest entrance, where antlers do duty as coat-hooks, leads into a galleried hall stuffed with objects. Sir George and Lady Monica look down from more-than-lifesize oils; a portrait of James VI leers from beneath the gallery; a heard of stags' heads juts sadly from walls and columns. The polished floor is littered with the relics of Sir George's big-game shooting. A Steinway grand dominates a shopful of Japanese lacquer cabinets, Indian brass-topped tables, marble-topped whatnots and arthritic chairs. There are Japanese vases 9ft high and a grandfather clock looms 12ft from the floor.

The airy dining-room, panelled in lozenges of polished mahogany, has french windows giving on to the terrace; its oval table is covered by a lawn cloth still set with napkins stamped *Rhouma*. The lofty ballroom looks on to the inner courtyard; in spite of a cream barrel-vault ceiling, cream panelling, gold wallpaper, gold curtains, gold-encrusted couches, and cream and gold chairs, the place looks cold and bare.

The billiard room with its club fender, leather armchairs and velvet curtains was the heart of the masculine domain, although no doubt the ladies watched play from an elevated viewing area, alongside some intimidating 11ft high black statuary. A framed pedigree traces the family back from the nineteenth century in Oswaldtwistle to the twelfth, in Fazackerley. There is a testimonial to John from his workers. There are red and blue daubs of local scenes which justify McCulloch's unkind description of Rum: 'most repulsive of all the islands'. Lady Monica's drawing room in the sunny south-east corner is the feminine heart of the house. French windows look down the Loch and up Hallival. A white moulded ceiling, panelled walls inlaid with flowered silk, olive carpet, chaises-longues and chairs in pink-and-white glazed chintz, elegant tables of inlaid mahogany and delicate lustred chandeliers combine to form a room lovely by any standards. One of the fireplaces is in an alcove which might have been designed for gossip, and probably was.

There is an Empire room in gold, white and red, complete with a painting of Napoleon; a library of 2,000 books (Scott, Dumas, Tolstoi, the Brigade of Guards Magazine and *The*

*Grouse in Health and in Diseases*); Lady Monica's surprisingly plain bedroom and Sir George's room with draped-silk bedhead of indescribable ugliness. There are the ponderous mahogany bath and shower units with arrays of taps like valves in an engineroom. There is the brass-piped Orchestrion, worked by compressed air, which plays selections from *Maritana, Lohengrin, The Geisha*. There are those risqué paintings (*L'Épouse Indiscrete, Les Bains du Diane, Lady Hamilton—a Great Friend of Lord Nelson*) and those disappointing books (*Ladies Fair and Frail, The Gilded Beauties of the Second Empire, My Past* by Css Marie Lariche).

The gardens are gone. Broken statues lie forlorn beside the island children's swings and slides. There was a large walled orchard. Palms and bamboos are said to have flourished. Peaches, nectarines, figs, grapes and bananas grew in the great glasshouses. Brilliant tropical birds flew freely in the immense conservatory. Water from the mouth of Kinloch River was heated and pumped to turtle ponds and reptile tanks, where young alligators thrived until the terrified staff prevailed on Sir George to remove them. The head gardener (from Alton Tower) had a staff of fourteen. The housekeeper had twenty-four. Rum's resident population rose from 53 in 1891 to 90 in 1901 and peaked at 94 in 1911, when there were two dozen children in school. Conditions of service were good; 'perks' included free meat, fish, milk and 5 tons of coal a year.

But strangers were not welcome. Rum became known as the Forbidden Island. Stories were told and lost nothing in the telling: innocent folk had been driven off at gunpoint, the island people were oppressed. This was nonsense, but there was real resentment all the same. For his part Sir George resented the insulting remarks about his castle and mausoleum which became almost obligatory in articles on the island. Throughout his time, MacBraynes advertised a service to Rum, but when the ferry came alongside only passengers having permission to do so were allowed to land; many little dramas were played out before an interested audience as the steamer swung with the tide. Yet had this been a mainland estate few would have objected to 'Private' on the gate. In 1934 two young journalists decided to assert the right of all true Scots to land on the Sassenach's island. Having canoed from the south they pitched tent conspicuously, were warned off, refused to leave and were summoned to the castle, where they received Lady Monica's compliments, permission to camp, and a haunch of venison. They had a 'sumptuous supper' at an 'oppressed' worker's cottage and were given sandwiches to sustain them on the long paddle to Mallaig; Alastair Dunnett, retired editor of *The Scotsman*, recalls that it was a tricky run, a large lump of venison being awkward cargo for a one-man canoe.

By then Rum had long been in decline. In its heyday, the ten years ending in 1913, the Bulloughs would winter at their Herefordshire house, hunting with the Ledbury; spring would see them at Warren Hall, Newmarket, for the racing; and in early summer Sir George would bring *Rhouma II* into Loch Scresort and entertain a houseful of guests until October. Nearly all were guards or cavalry officers, their wives and lady-friends; Sir George's half-brother, Ian, brought Lily Elsie, the stage beauty (whom he was later to marry) and, according to tradition, the Gaiety Girls came too. A sea-worn stone lies in the porch of the now dark and silent house. On it there is an inscription: 'This stone was carried from Guiridil Beach by Captain Webber April 2nd 1903. Weight 17lb.' It reads like an epitaph for a world long dead.

No deer were shot in 1914; the guards and cavalry had other targets. Major Sir George Bullough left to superintend a Remount Depot. *Rhouma II* went on naval patrol. The central heating plant ran cool and the tropical birds died off. The turtles were let loose into the sea—their stranding on mainland beaches caused speculation in the Scottish press. Sir George left the Remount Depot in 1916, and was raised to baronet. In the post-war years the Bulloughs came to Rum by mailboat, and only for the shooting season; the gardens were largely abandoned and the glasshouses fell into decay.

In 1932 their only child, Hermione, who dearly loved the island (and still does) married the 5th Earl of Durham. Rum's population fell as old employees left; by 1936 it was down to twenty.

Sir George died of heart failure whilst out playing golf near Boulogne in July 1939 and the island passed to Trustees. After the war Lady Monica, still a smart and beautiful woman, came up occasionally from her London flat to join small shooting parties. On her last visit in 1954, at the age of eighty-five, she drove her old Austin up the boulder-strewn track from Kinloch, over the shoulder at Ard Nev and down the sweeping hairpin bends to Harris Bay, where Sir George and his father lay in their lonely temple. Next time she passed that way it was a cold and wet day in May 1967, and she came to join her husband. She had died, in London, aged ninety-eight.

# 10  NATURAL HISTORY

In Rum thre were formerly great numbers of deer . . . now
that the wood is destroyed, the deer are extirpated . . . the
method of killing deer was as follows . . . stone dykes were . . .
carried to the lower part of the valley, always drawing
nearer, till within 3 or 4 feet of each other. From this narrow
pass, a circular space was enclosed by a stone wall . . . to this
place they were pursued, and destroyed.

THAT account was written in the 1790s. Deforesting
alone would not have 'extirpated' red deer; around
1845 Lord Salisbury re-established them on an almost
treeless island. John Bullough made later introductions from
Meggernie and Windsor. There were fallow deer in his time,
but they died out.

The islands' domestic goats went feral when replaced by
sheep and cattle in the eighteenth and nineteenth centuries.
Goats had gone from Coll and Tiree by the 1920s, though
surviving on Gunna in 1934. They were re-introduced to
Eigg in 1913 and around 1930 when forty animals roamed
the Sgurr ridge; they died out in the harsh winter of 1946–7.
About a score remain on Canna. The hundred or so on
Rum's southern seacliffs, which have successfully resisted
attempts at reduction, may descend from domestic stock
recorded in the 1770s, or from Edwardian introductions.

Wolves are recalled by *Leana Uilbh*, ('meadow of the
wolf') near Gallanach, Coll, foxes by Fox's Rock on Eigg and
badgers by an Eigg story of a hunter killed at Struidh 'with
an otter and a badger, the produce of his day's toil'. Otters
breed on all the islands; in the 1960s Eigg's boatman had one

which trotted happily at the end of a dog-lead, and ultimately went to Gavin Maxwell. There are rabbits on Eigg, Canna and Coll, despite myxomotosis, and a menace they are to crops on the machair, although originally introduced as a food source. In Edwardian times Eigg crofters exported the skins. They were on Canna in 1793—'of a greyish colour'— and in 1887, 'white'. The Coll breed was 'all black' at the end of the nineteenth century and 'black and lavender' in the 1930s. They were on Tiree in 1793, extinct by 1840, re-introduced later, but 'lamentably conspicuous by their absence' by the 1890s.

Hares imported to Coll about 1785 had increased to many hundreds seven years later; they were introduced to Tiree about 1820 and are still present on both islands. Brought to Eigg in the 1890s and present on Rum until 1917, hares are now unkown on Small Isles. Brown rats haunt the beaches by night, feeding on shellfish and harassing gull and tern colonies by sucking eggs and eating young, notably on Gunna. They burrow in starling dung in caves at Ceann a Mhara, Tiree. John Bullough's Rum keeper reported them 'nearly extinct', having killed 4,000 between 1881 and 1886. Short-tailed voles, pigmy shrews and Hebridean field mice are widely distributed; Rum and Eigg sub-species of the latter were once distinguished. House mice are unknown on Eigg, Rum and Muck. There are bats on Eigg, Rum, Coll and Tiree. Adders are absent from the six islands, perhaps proving Columban visits. Frogs and toads are not found on all islands, but lizards and newts are common.

There are breeding colonies of grey seals on Gunna (87 in 1970), Heiskeir (45 in 1971) and Canna (normally 30–40), and a few are born each year on Horse Island, Muck. In calm weather seals haul out along most coasts—conspicuously around Eigg, Canna and Muck harbours and on Eilean Mor, Cairns of Coll. It was probably on Heiskeir that young Donald MacNeill of Canna shot a grey seal weighing 45 stones, for a profitable annual culling took place there in the nineteenth century. Common seals are often seen below

Caenn a Mhara. Both species abound off Tiree beaches and can be attracted by singing to their scout.

## BIRDS

Of the mainland species, 40 per cent occur on Eigg (excluding vagrants), 39 per cent on Rum, 35 per cent on Coll and Tiree, 31 per cent on Muck and 30 per cent on Canna. Over 200 species have been identified on the islands. There are usually three or four breeding pairs of golden eagle on Rum, two on Eigg and two on Canna; birds have reconnoitred Muck. Bullough's ratting keeper killed five pairs around 1886, but the species recolonised. Although the Laig Mac-Donalds kept a captive golden eagle in 1845, Eigg's first breeding pair was recorded at Sron na h-Iolaire as late as 1930—the name indicates earlier use by the larger white-tailed species. The latter bred on Eigg (Sgurr to 1833, Clea-dale cliffs to 1877), Canna (north-west cliffs to 1875, a vagrant seen in 1920) and Rum (eight killed 1866, the last pair 1907) where Nature Conservancy are currently attempting re-intro-duction by importing caged Norwegian eaglets. Buzzards breed on all islands except Rum, which lacks rabbits, their favourite food; Tiree birds eat leverets and young seabirds.

There are Manx shearwaters on Eigg, Rum and Canna. These black-and-white birds with scimitar wings commonly winter in South America and return in spring to burrows in steep slopes; a pair may occupy the same one year after year. Whilst one bird sits, the other spends the day at sea, returning with food by night. Rafts of several thousand may be seen from the mailboat. Sixty thousand or more pairs have burrows 1,500–2,000ft up along Rum's Barkeval–Hallival–Askival–Trollaval ridge in shearwater greens made fertile by droppings which stabilise the slopes. Until the 1930s Eigg's colony on the inland cliffs at Laig Cuagach and Cleadale extended right round the east side; but by 1964 numbers were reportedly down to fifty pairs, at Cleadale. Latterly there has been considerable recovery.

A night on Eigg's airy shearwater slopes is one to remember. The sun sets over Rum. The night silence, edged by the thin splash of an unseen waterfall, is broken by the first faint call of a homing bird—*cock-a-row, cock-a-row*—echoing off cliffs towering into a misty sky. Calls increase in number and volume until the dark air seems filled with them. Suddenly, alarmingly, a bird flies close, and one feels the pressure-change induced by its wings as it jinks away with a banshee howl. Birds land at their burrows with a heavy thud. A murmuring rises from the ground. No wonder Norsemen gave the name 'Trollaval', mountain of the goblins, to a Rum peak where shearwaters still nest. The clamour continues all night, rising to quick crescendos, falling to sudden silences. As one descends from the heights it can still be heard from Eigg's main road, but when the cold mono-chrome of dawn outlines the high tops of Rum the shear-waters' strange song gives way to the piping of oystercatchers scampering on the shore, and the rasp of a corncrake from the hayfields.

Rats and otters were probably responsible for the reduction in Eigg's shearwaters, and the former now occupy many old burrows. Although rats forage at these lower levels all the year round, they seem not to reach the higher Rum colonies until after the birds have migrated. Yet shearwater colonies low on the northern cliffs of Canna and beside the track to Tarbert are thriving; 1,000-plus pairs were present in the 1960s. *Fachach*, the Gaelic name for shearwater, is (or was) a nickname for any native of Eigg. Young birds used to be salted down and stewed for winter food; they taste like veal.

Several hundred puffins nested at Grulins, Eigg, until the early 1950s and they still breed on the other Small Isles. Fulmars breed on all the islands. Since 1963 they have colonised Eigg's south-western cliffs—the island's lack of other seabird colonies may be due to these, its only major seacliffs, being exposed to prevailing south-westerly gales. Two hundred pairs breed around Dibidil, Rum, and 600 have been counted on near-vertical cliffs at Ceann a Mhara,

Tiree. Ceann a Mhara in the breeding season is a sight to see. Fulmars sit tight on heady ledges bright with sea thrift, vetches, crimson clover and wild geraniums. Kittiwakes crouch in vertical clefts, tier on tier, seemingly on nothing at all. Razorbills inhabit crazy overhangs. Brown young shags, big as their parents, lie flat as flukes on nests spattered up the sides of a geo and inside a dark and craggy cave where only the white of their opened beaks is visible. Far below a cliff-top purple with wild thyme, the green sea boils and hisses.

Barnacle and white-fronted geese and whooper swans winter on Tiree, and the greylag breeds on Coll. The mild winters attract them from a colder mainland; Loch a Phuill and Loch Bhasapoll are alive with their movement. Winter sees huge numbers of snipe on Tiree, one of the finest shoots in Britain; 37,000 were killed there between 1929 and 1955 of which 2,000 were jack-snipe. They breed on all the islands. The maximum shoot on Eigg was 114 in 1934–5, when 200 woodcock were killed, a figure which rose to 600 in the winter of 1939–40.

John Bullough introduced pheasants to Rum in the 1880s; they roosted among the heather and seemed 'quite at home' for a time. Commander MacEwen tried them on Muck in 1922 but they had gone eight years later, and they also failed on Canna; 200–400 were shot yearly on Eigg in the 1930s and several pairs are still seen. Pheasants and partridges have increased on Coll. Red grouse, plentiful before the last war, died out there in the 1960s, perhaps because heather had been burnt and over-grazed, but they were recently introduced at Arivirig, opposite Arinagour. There are about fifty pairs of grouse on Rum and a dozen on Eigg.

## TREES

Timber in the peat shows that the islands once had many trees, although on poor soils like Rum's they were probably rather scrubby. Rum deer were formerly forest creatures (see p 118); woodland fungi *Agaricus langei* grow there on cliff sites now lacking all cover. Deforestation—perhaps for Norse or later ship-building, perhaps to supply seventeenth-century mainland ironworks—was completed when fuel became short in the era of overcrowding. In 1790–1 Muck folk were reduced to burning 'beds, dressers, stools, barrels and also house-timber'.

Re-afforestation by the people was out of the question; they had neither capital nor security. When in 1803 the 5th Duke planted 'forest trees' on Tiree 'the natives . . . pulled up almost every one'. Belief that trees would not or should not grow persisted despite the sycamores at Laig and Howlin, Eigg; Dr Maclean's sycamore ash and beech at Kinloch, Rum; the MacPhersons' forestry on Eigg and thriving trees in the Coll factor's garden; as late as 1889 'crofters had their own ways' with 3 acres of *pinus maritimus* seedlings on Ben Hough, Tiree. The huge Eucalypts at Eigg Lodge, 6oft Sitka Spruce in Muck's exposed plantations, and the West of Scotland Agricultural College trial plot at Kirkapoll, Tiree, show what can be done, but high extraction costs inhibit commercial forestry.

### FLOWERS

The title 'Island of Flowers' has been applied to most of the islands. The floral variety and profusion, the sheer exuberant colour of the high-summer machair has to be seen to be believed. One can wade knee-deep in flowers. Westerly breezes carry the scent of Breachacha fields across to the car-ferry as she passes 2 miles offshore. Professor Heslop Harrison's Durham University expeditions during the 1930s–40s found 651 forms of flowering plants 'and their closest allies' on Small Isles, 573 on Coll and Tiree. Those numbers, since added to, may be compared with around 600 for the whole of the Outer Hebrides. Nature Conservancy's probably more thorough count on Rum is 427.

Harrison explained exotic finds by controversial hypotheses. Pipewort (*Eriocaulon septangulare*) in Coll lochs, the Irish

Ladies Tresses orchid (*Spiranthes Romanzoffiam (stricta)*) on moorland between Cliad and Sorisdale, and Blue-eyed Grass (*Sisyrinchium angustifolium*) on the south-east margin of Loch Cliad, taken together with the presence on both Coll and Tiree of the Irish race of the Greasy Fritillary butterfly (*Euphydryas aurinia* var *praeclara*) and on Gunna of the Irish Burnet (*Zygoena purpuralis*) led him to conclude that Coll and Tiree and perhaps Small Isles had a 'more or less recent' land connection with the southern Outer Isles and Northern Ireland—where these species, generally absent from the mainland, are found. Distributions like the Hebridean bee (*Bombus smithianus*), found in the southern Outer Isles, Heiskeir and Eigg, but absent on Mull and the mainland, were accounted for not by a retreat westwards before more successful species, but by a retreat eastwards from land sunk beneath the Atlantic ('the Tir fo thonn of Gaelic legend'). Alpine Pennycross (*Thlaspi calaminare*) on Fionchra and Bloodstone, Rum; Norwegian sandwort (*Arenaria norvegica*) among the Coolins; Pyramidal bugle (*Ajuga pyramidalis*) on the Beinn Bhuidhe cliffs and south-west moorland of Eigg, on Muck, and on rock ledges on Coll, and other alpine plants usually associated with unglaciated localities, were thought to indicate that higher parts of the islands escaped glaciation, although not necessarily those were the plants are now found. Less expert observers merely rejoice in a glorious June show of alpines like Mountain Avens, Mossy Saxifrage, Globe Flower and Cushion Pink.

25 Farming: *(above)* cattle can just be made out on the Atlantic surf beach, Ballevullin, Tiree *(R. Petrie)*;
26 *(below)* croftland on Sanday, Canna, with Compass Hill beyond *(Adam Collection)*

27 Peace and plenty: *(above)* fishing boat on the placid shores of Gunna
Sound, Caoles, Tiree;
28 *(below)* a Canna fisherman makes his creels *(Violet Banks)*

# 11 COMMUNICATIONS

THE six islands were near Columba's Iona, on the route from Norway to Man, and close to the Lords of the Isles' headquarters at Ardtornish; but for half a millennium they have been on the edge of a communications system based on Edinburgh and London.

## ROADS TO THE ISLES

Around 1800 Reginald George Clanranald and other land-owners put up £1,500 to build a road from Arisaig to Fort William, but this was equivalent to only 2½p a linear yard and work soon stopped. In 1803 Telford, engineer to the Highland Roads and Bridges Commissioners, put the work out to contract for £6,900, to be paid equally by Commissioners and landowners. The job had its troubles. Local men were reluctant to work for the going rate of 7½p per day. All skilled stonemasons were on the Caledonian Canal. The Arisaig priest spread a rumour that the contractor was bankrupt and the men downed tools. When the Commissioners finished the road in 1812 they had difficulty in extracting payment from Clanranald, who was 'very coolly and quietly playing the devil in London'. Although McCulloch thought it a '*plusquam perfectum* road . . . like a gravel walk in a garden', there was no ferry from Arisaig and it was scarcely used. Caulfield took the Oban road as far as Taynuilt before 1767, but it was not extended to Oban until 1832.

## SAILING SHIPS

When Knox of the Fisheries Society visited Tiree in 1786 he

wrote 'whoever goes [to the Hebrides] must engage a vessel for thirty or forty pounds a month without proper accommodation, and even without bedding'. He crossed to Coll by the Caoles ferry which the minister thought dangerous 'owing to . . . rapid currents and amazing breakers'. Coll had a packet to Tobermory and Tiree had ten smacks, but 'the only boat in which any person except those amphibious animals the Highland fishers would venture himself . . . was away' and Knox left on a 'foreign' vessel. In 1801 the Tiree factor established a 60-ton sloop with monopoly rights in kelp and barley, and a weekly packet to Croig Mull, but neither survived the kelping slump.

### VICTORIAN STEAMERS AND ROUTES

Napier's *Highland Chieftain* sailed from Glasgow to Isle Ornsay, Skye, in 1820 but it was many years before the six islands had their own calls. Hutcheson-MacBrayne's *Clansman* provided Eigg's first recorded service in 1857 on a 'request-stop' basis—she flew her flag half-mast to summon the ferry. Their 1855 summer timetable had a heading 'Coll and Tiree', but the entry is illegible, and the first-known regular call was by Martin Orme's *Islesman* in 1862. Four years later both islands had a weekly summer service. Captain John McCallum's *Hebridean* was serving Rum 'by special arrangement' in 1882.

Early services sailed from the Clyde, but during the 1860s MacBrayne started a summer run from Oban (connecting with the mailcoach) which called alternately at Arisaig and Eigg. When the railway reached Oban in 1881 he put on a year-round run to Outer Isles and Skye, serving Coll and Tiree and Eigg or Arisaig. From the 1870s a Fort William–Arisaig mail-gig called at Glenfinnan, Lochailort ('poor little inn') and Arisaig Hotel ('most commendable, good clean and moderate—English landlord'), but when the railway reached Fort William in 1894 the road had deteriorated, vehicles would not venture beyond Glenfinnan and a mailcoach took eight hours to cover the 40 miles. After being guaranteed 3 per cent, given £45,000 for a breakwater (still not built) and virtually exempted from rates, the West Highland Railway opened the Mallaig Extension in 1901—the only subsidised line built in Britain.

The Oban and Mallaig railheads shortened sea passages which could still be difficult. Edward Stanford, the Tiree industrialist:

> the nearest bank was at Tobermory . . . further off than California in winter. At imminent risk of life I had frequently to go there in a smack . . . and [have] been two days between Tobermory and Tiree . . . A clerk sent out from Glasgow . . . with £300 returned with it about three weeks afterwards; he had seen almost every . . . island except the one he was sent to.

Frederick Rea, a teacher travelling to South Uist in December 1899 on *Staffa*, booked to call at Coll and Tiree:

> We were passing between two low, sandy, windswept islands. Soon I noticed one of the few passengers wildly gesticulating stamping and shouting . . . he wanted to buy cattle and sheep on those two islands . . . the sea was too rough for boats to come out . . . this was the third successive week that he had made the round . . . his hopes being defeated each time by heavy seas.

Some idea of routes and steamers over the years is given in Appendix C.

### TWENTIETH-CENTURY SHIPPING SERVICES

Many unkind things are said about island transport, but the prime difficulty—the expense of serving such tiny communities—is seldom mentioned:

| *Populations* | *1851* | *1951* |
|---|---|---|
| Hebrides (as percentage of Scotland) | 3·0 | 1·2 |
| Six islands (as percentage of the Hebrides) | 6·6 | 2·7 |

The glories of Eigg's Edwardian services are still remembered: 'ten fast paddle-steamers a week, apart from cargo vessels'. So many calls must have been a nuisance—when would the ferrymen have time for their crofts? The service ran for three summer months and for the rest of the year there were four calls a week. Coll and Tiree enjoyed their own run from Oban terminating at Bunessan, Mull, but after World War I they shared a steamer with Barra and South Uist and their calls were frequently 'missed'. MacBrayne's ageing postwar fleet left much to be desired. Mary Donaldson, author and well-known visitor to the Hebrides, on *Cygnet*:

> This remarkably comfortless boat is a floating slum. [I was] routed out of one of the sixteen berths in the pokey cabin . . . so that the officers might breakfast . . . to seek what accommodation was available among the cargo and cattle in the unsavoury hold.

*Cygnet*, built in 1904 to carry cargo in sheltered waters, served island passengers until 1930. MacBrayne's failed to regain tourist trade lost during the 1914–18 war and in 1928 their shares were acquired by Coast Lines and the LMS railway, which with £50,000 annual subsidy formed David MacBrayne (1928), which built *Lochearn* and *Lochmor*, 452-ton sister ships. *Lochearn* ran Oban–Coll–Tiree–South Uist, out one day back the next; *Lochmor* ran Mallaig–Eigg–Rum–Canna–South Uist–Harris–Kyle–Mallaig or reverse, three times a week; these services survived until 1964. Cargo runs from the Clyde were made by McCallum Orme to Coll and Tiree, and by MacBraynes to Small Isles. MacBraynes acquired McCallum Orme in 1948 and replaced Coll and Tiree's cargo boats *Hebrides* (fifty years old) and *Dunara Castle* (seventy-three!)

Rocketing subsidies led to economy drives in which Rum and Canna lost their cargo call in 1949 and Eigg in 1952. In 1955 *Claymore*, a handsome 1,000-tonner, replaced *Lochearn* on the Coll and Tiree run and on 6 May 1964 *Lochmor* made her last call at Small Isles. She was the finest ship that ever served them or ever will. Her hold could take 120 lambs or 35 head of cattle. She had comfortable cabins, an elegant panelled dining-room, a lounge furnished in prim uncut-moquette and a leather-and-mahogany saloon redolent of whisky and cigars.

Her successor, *Loch Arkaig,* a 179-ton wooden inshore minesweeper given a lightweight superstructure when Mac-Braynes bought her in 1959, has no hold and no covered accommodation for livestock. When she started Small Isles' run she had no ferry door. Her lounge is reminiscent of a seaside-promenade shelter; only tea and buns are available. She does a circuit of Small Isles four times a week. On summer Saturdays there was formerly a 'double-run' which allowed two hours ashore in Mallaig. This invaluable arrangement—Small Islanders' only chance to shop in Mallaig without staying overnight—ceased in 1976.

*Claymore* was replaced in 1972 by the 1,089-ton *Loch Seaforth* of 1947, a fine ship taking sixteen cars. On the calm misty night of 22 March 1973 she hit a rock in Gunna Sound. Her captain, crew and twelve passengers (less one left asleep!) made Gott in two boats. Refloated, she was towed to Gott where she sank alongside the pier on the 23rd. No other vessel could get in. Ferrying was restored, the Tiree stocksales were cancelled and, after indignation meetings and telegrams of protest, she was raised on 14 May by a floating crane from the Rhine, and towed away for breaking. *Claymore* returned, shortly to be replaced by *Iona,* a 1,192-ton fifty-car ferry which lacked sleeping accommodation (handy for the 6.00 am start from Oban); this having been provided, the 2,104-ton car ferry *Columba* took over. Of late there has been a direct summer service four times a week, and a thrice-weekly one, also serving Castlebay and South Uist, for the rest of the year.

Since 1969 Hebridean transport has been organised—if that is the right word—by the Scottish Transport Group; under the Transport Act 1968 'uneconomic' services like those run by MacBraynes (now nationalised) to the six islands are meant to receive local authority support. Coll and Tiree's services seem secure but Small Isles' lacks certainty now the ageing *Arkaig* no longer plies to Raasay, and is almost wholly charged against Small Isles' run. The future of *Loch Carron*, said to be the only vessel available for Small Isles' annual livestock runs to Oban, is also in doubt, for her weekly cargo service—which includes Coll and Tiree—has been declared 'redundant'. (Loch Carron was sold in 1976.)

In the winter of 1973–4 MacBraynes' tiny car-ferry *Coll* served Small Isles, but she could not show her nose out of Mallaig in a force 4 wind, and the service was the worst for a century. In March 1975 Small Isles' representatives reached agreement with MacBraynes on a successor to *Arkaig*: a 250-ton boat to stern-load 8 cars, 2 lorries, or equivalent livestock, and take 58 winter and 170 summer passengers, 'subject to government approval and money being made available'. A new daily summer service from Arisaig to Eigg was started in 1976 by Arisaig Marine Ltd, using an excellently converted naval launch. *Shearwater*'s double-run on Saturdays gives Eigg folk two hours ashore in Arisaig.

Eigg's proprietor has a Sea-Truck workboat which can take livestock off beaches.

### PIERS AND FERRIES

'A Highland quay is a quarter of a mile from the sea at low water and completely submerged at high tide.' Eigg's Clanranald pier meets Stanford's specification reasonably well: founded on a pitchstone dyke, it was built about 1790 by statute labour. Government grants following the potato famine may account for the old piers at Kinloch, Rum, and Arinagour, Coll, and for the jetties at Heanish and Balephuil, Tiree. Scarinish pier dates from around 1771 when the land on which it stands, formerly an island, was connected by causeway to the 'mainland'. None of these structures sufficed for scheduled steamer services, which take no account of tides. Small vessels could get in to Scarinish or even Arinagour at high water, but ferrying became the normal rule. *Dunara*

*Castle* arriving off Scarinish in 1886: 'A large boat, with three men at each of the four oars, came out . . . and into it were tumbled pell-mell men women and tables, and bags of coal, and loaves of bread, and boxes.' (The plethora of oarsmen was due to the presence of a bar on the steamer and the absence of that amenity on Tiree.)

Robert Thom obtained a Canna Pier Order in 1892 and built a greenheart structure before the end of the century (replaced in reinforced concrete in 1937). Tiree waited rather longer. Captain Pim who charted island waters in the 1870s priced a pier in Gott Bay at £6,000; Stanford thought £12,000 might be needed and had 'no doubt that a pier could be made . . . on the very stiff clay' but 'eminent engineers' engaged by the 8th Duke would not 'guarantee a pier would stand'. That opinion was not shared by Lady Victoria Campbell, whose pier campaign gathered force when the Tiree ferry capsized in November 1891, fortunately without loss of life. A government grant seems to have been offered (although in 1902 the Scottish Office thought 'no sane individual or Corporation will undertake . . . maintenance') and vociferous support was provided after the 1905 Glasgow holiday when bad weather marooned several hundred Glaswegians for a week and lost some of them their jobs. The project was again delayed for want of a guarantor, although 'dues would make the investment a splendid one', according to the parish minister; and visitors objected that a pier would allow motor cars to invade their occasional paradise.

Gott Bay pier was started in 1909 and opened in 1914, having cost £25,000. It was partially rebuilt after both wars and taken over by Argyll County Council in 1951, when dues were abolished; new cattle penning was provided in 1976 but congestion and a 7·5 ton limit point to further reconstruction. Tiree thus achieved a steamer pier fifty-four years after its first recorded steamer service.

Coll, which had a rowing-boat ferry into the 1930s, waited over a century. A fine wide pier with waiting-room, cattle pens and fluorescent lighting opened in 1967. Two years later Campbell of Canna, told that *Loch Carron* could not get in for his cattle and sheep, promptly broadened, widened and deepened his pier and built a vehicle slipway; not a penny of public money has ever been spent on Canna pier.

Eigg, Rum and Muck are the only sizeable Hebridean communities still served by ferry, with all its attendant disadvantages and expense. The moving of hospital cases and beasts for market presents particular difficulties. Modern packaging is vulnerable to hasty handling and wet conditions, while the trans-shipment of Eigg and Muck's diesel and petrol in 40-gallon drums, which weigh nearly a quarter of a ton, is no joke even in calm conditions. Fortunately all three islands have stout diesel-ferryboats. Eigg's belongs to MacBraynes and is licensed 'to ply between ship and shore . . . in fair weather and between sunrise and sunset': Roddy Campbell, whose family have run Eigg ferry since the 1890s, has to interpret those words widely on occasion.

An expensive survey for a pier at Kildonnan, Eigg, was made in the late 1960s, and a commitment to survey one for Muck must still be in the army's list of operations in aid of Scottish civil authorities (OPMAC). Meanwhile Eigg has a dilapidated stone structure, reputedly built by Thomson, to which Inverness-shire County Council added an underwater obstacle, quaintly called a 'pier extension'. Rum has an aptly named concrete slipway, and Muck has Port Mor jetty 'built by the inhabitants circa 1830 and later partly reconstructed', according to the Listed Building returns.

## SEAMARKS AND LIFEBOATS

The Skerryvore, Ardnamurchan and Heiskeir lights date from 1844, 1849 and 1904; they now have foghorns and radio beacons. Skerryvore and Heiskeir are 'rock' stations; three keepers from the Oban depot are always stationed at each. Skerryvore's base was at Erraid and Heiskeir's at Canna into the 1930s. Servicing is by tender, but since 1973 crew-changing has been by helicopter. Automatic lights were provided at Scarinish in 1897, Castle Island, Eigg, in 1906, Canna in 1907, Suil Ghorm, Cairns of Coll, in 1909 and Point of Sleat, Skye, as late as 1933.

The lifeboat station at Tobermory closed owing to manning difficulties in 1948, when the Mallaig station opened. Other local stations are at Castlebay and Port Askaig, Islay. An RAF rescue helicopter is shortly to be based at Tiree airfield.

*Skerryvore light*

> Eternal granite hewn from the living isle
> And dowelled with brute iron, rears a tower
> That from its wet foundation to its crown
> Of glittering glass, stands, in the sweep of winds,
> Immovable, immortal, eminent.

Robert Louis Stevenson knew Skerryvore—although he was wrong about the dowelling. In 1834 his uncle Alan Stevenson, the engineer, charted 140 rocks of Lewisian gneiss polished glass-smooth by ice, their hollows filled by concretionary bird-lime. Landing was 'like climbing up the side of a bottle'. In 1800–40 thirty ships are known to have struck Skerryvore and twenty subsequently came ashore between Hough Bay and Hynish, Tiree. A recent survey revealed thirty old wrecks around the lighthouse tower.

In July 1840 the 7th Duke of Argyll, his Duchess, Lord Lorne and 'a party of ladies and gentlemen' came to Skerryvore. They trans-shipped from their steamer well away from the lighthouse site. 'A small boat,' Lorne wrote, 'rowing amidst the heavings and swellings of the Atlantic is incompatible with any feeling of security' but they landed safely, though 'there did not seem one square foot . . . even tolerably level'. Alan Stevenson was living with his men in a timber barrack 15ft in diameter and 30ft high, held 30ft above the sea by four massive rakers (imagine a birdcage on top of a wigwam); an earlier barrack had been swept away. Having laid a foundation-stone and taken pot-shots at 'a great gray seal—a rare species' the party got thankfully away.

Tiree gneiss was difficult to work, and the 150ft tower is

of Erraid granite. Its light was lit on 1 February 1844 and was seen from Barra Head, 38 miles away. Not a single life was lost in its building.

*Skerryvore works on Tiree*

Alan Stevenson's advance party arrived at 3 am on 24 June 1838 'but this day being Sunday, no work was done'. Ultimately a hundred men were employed at Hynish depot. Many brought their families, and some are buried in Soroby graveyard. They built their own barracks and set up their own shop. They shaped the stone into blocks, fitted and numbered them and shipped them to Skerryvore. Hynish is still dominated by their magnificent masonry. Stone workshops face a pier 100yd long by 10yd wide (91 × 9m) and a 40 × 15yd (36 × 14m) basin built to serve the ship linking Hynish with the lighthouse site 12 miles away. Loving care and unimaginable toil went into the massive pink-granite blockwork, the sharp straight arrises, and the stone bollards that look like new. The flat-roofed keepers' houses on Barradhu ridge with their ponderous porches, tall chimneys and walled gardens must be among the best ever provided for working people in early Victorian times—they even had piped water. They face a circular signalling-tower from which contact was maintained with the light.

Both pier and basin tended to silt-up. A flushing device (stream water was stored in a stone culvert) proved unsuccessful and the keepers were moved to Erraid. Hynish was one of the earliest steamer piers in the Hebrides, but its failure provided the 8th Duke with a reason for not providing one elsewhere.

### AIR SERVICES

In 1934 John Sword of Midland and Scottish Airways selected a landing strip on The Reef, Tiree. DH Tiger Moths started a Glasgow–Glenbrittle, Skye, service in 1935 that was meant to call at Reef, but a dispute about rental delayed the start of a daily summer service until 1937. The Glasgow–Tiree service continued with some intermittency during World War II, when a civil grass strip remained open alongside the huge RAF field. British European Airways took over in 1947, using Dakotas from 1951 and DH Herons from 1955, on a route now Glasgow–Tiree–Barra. Tiresians recall their elegant four-propeller Herons with affection; they had a touch of luxury rare in island transport. In 1973 twin-propeller Short Skyliners took over, but high noise levels and running costs caused them to be replaced in 1974 by Loganair's three-propeller sixteen-seater Britten–Norman Trislanders.

RAF Reef was larger than Abbotsinch, but much land is now leased for grazing; 954yd (868m) of concrete and 1,158yd (1,054m) and 392yd (356m) of black-top runways remain usable. Pavement strengths limit the acceptable aircraft; the largest to land in recent years were Andovers bringing fuel during the 1972 dockers' strike. Reef's beacon gives slope/direction indication through 360°, and the limiting factor on landing is commonly visual ground-contact. Aircraft for Coll and Barra home on Reef beacon and maintain visual contact thereafter. Low cloud results in the service 'missing' Tiree perhaps four times a year. Reef has gooseneck flares for air ambulance work but is not licensed for night flying; the Civil Aviation Authority maintains a staff of eleven, including ambulancemen and firemen/loaders, under a traffic controller /manager.

Current schedules, which are subsidised, give four Glasgow–Tiree flights a week used by upwards of 4,000 passengers a year. Flights may be a trifle bumpy because of the many land–sea crossings and the 10,000ft ceiling for unpressurised aircraft, but the journey can be a joy, the views from around 5,000ft being superb on a cloudless day. The service 'floor' is 3,700ft to clear Ben More, Mull.

In 1968 an army OPMAC operation improved Coll's Totronald air-ambulance strip to licensing standards, a crash/rescue trailer was provided and charter flights commenced. A summer service Glasgow–Mull–Coll–Tiree started in 1970, the first scheduled transport to the six islands ever to operate on Sundays. Permission to use Reef on the sabbath was, however, withdrawn and from 1971 the service, confined to summer weekends, terminated at Coll. The eight-seat twin-propeller Britten–Norman Islanders—which took 80 minutes from Glasgow—were heavily subsidised and ceased to operate in 1975. Loganair has reconnoitred airstrip sites for islanders at Kildonnan, Eigg (on the list of OPMAC tasks) and Creag Liath, Canna. Nothing suitable was found on Rum, and Muck was not investigated. At Easter 1975 Keith Schellenberg, Eigg's proprietor, used a field behind Kildonnan for a smart single-engined three-seater which needs only about 100yd of level grass; proving flights were made from Aberdeen, Glasgow, Oban and Arisaig. Small Isles' folk may benefit greatly if this unexpected development is continued.

## POSTS

'We were in a strange state of abstraction from the world' wrote Boswell, on Coll in 1773. 'We could neither hear from our friends, nor write to them. It gave me much uneasiness to think of the anxiety my wife must suffer.' In the 1780s Alexander Maclean had a horse-post from Glasgow. From 1789 Coll mails came from Tobermory post office by packet, and in 1801 a Tiree packet from Croig Mull was receiving a PO grant of £5. Coll and Tiree had post offices in 1836 but the sea crossings were then 'at private expense'.

Small Isles long depended on Arisaig PO, established after the road to Fort William opened in 1812. Kenneth MacLeod, the Eigg poet, writing of the mid-nineteenth century:

> A smack crossed from the Island of Eigg to the mainland once in the week, weather and inclination permitting, for the few letters and one newspaper brought by stage-coach from Fort William to Arisaig: about a fortnight later, somebody sailed across from Rum to Eigg to see if any letters had arrived . . . in the course of another week, more or less, a shepherd from the west side of Rum, looking for stray sheep,

unexpectedly found himself in the seaport clachan of Kinloch, and while there might remember to ask if there were any letters for the neighbouring island of Canna; on the following day the folk of Canna saw a fire on a certain hill in Rum . . . and some time before the end of the week somebody who probably never in his life received a letter sailed across the Sound and returned with the mail-bag as soon as he felt in the mood for returning.

Visitors took a different view. Packenham Edgeworth, on Eigg in 1863: 'I have chartered a boat to go to Arisaig for letters tomorrow as I cannot stand any longer this entire silence from the rest of the world.' In the late 1860s letters for Eigg were addressed 'To the Clerk of the *Clansman* Steam Packet, c/o Custom House Greenock . . . for Post Master Arisaig'. Coll and Tiree's mails arrived by sailing packet from Tobermory until well into the 1870s and Stanford complained bitterly about the service. On 11 December 1863 he received a letter dater 17 November requiring a patent annuity to be paid by 3 December; the patent lapsed. On 26 December he received a tax assessment dated 18 November requiring any appeal to be submitted by 2 December; although he posted a cheque on 28 December, he got a final demand on 20 February.

There are currently four posts a week to Eigg, Rum and Canna; Muck collects from Eigg. Coll has three a week in winter and four in summer. Tiree enjoys an airmail service, but 'return of first class post' from England to the other islands can take over a fortnight.

### TELECOMMUNICATIONS

Reporters covering Tiree's 1886 War found the nearest telegraph office was Tobermory; one of them even tried pigeon-post. Morse telegraphy reached Tiree and Coll in 1888, and by the 1920s sub-post offices could pass telegrams to Tobermory by voice. From 1932 Coll and Tiree sub-post-office instruments were available for public calls to Mull. Coll had trunk calls from 1938, Tiree—packed with homesick airfield construction workers—in 1941.

A telegraph cable was laid from Skye to Eigg, Rum and Canna in 1899 (still subsidised by the Board of Agriculture in 1921). Telephones arrived in the 1930s but only Eigg subscribers could get beyond Fort William; Rum's booked calls averaged one a week, Canna's three a year. A magneto exchange opened in 1940 but arrangements were far from perfect; in the 1950s Canna callers were commonly 'reduced to a state of utter incoherence and rage trying to converse intelligibly with London or Glasgow' and much money went on telegrams. Telephones replaced smoke-signals on Muck in 1956. There is some social loss when the switchboard gives way to the impersonal dial. Eigg manual exchange closed in 1972, almost the last magneto installation in Britain. Tiree closed in November 1974 when STD came to its 164 subscribers and to Coll. In January 1976 Small Isles went STD and radio links connecting the six islands to Oban became almost fully operational.

In 1923 the post office installed a portable wireless at Scarinish when the telegraph cable broke. It 'aroused much interest' and was probably the first receiver on the islands. Radio and TV are important in these isolated places but reception has always been poor, although Small Isles' improved during daytime when the Skye station opened in 1965. ITV, BBC2 and colour transmissions are not available but BBC colour may reach Coll and Tiree before the end of the decade.

## ISLAND ROADS

'After a little amendment,' Tiree's minister remarked in 1794, the island roads would be 'ideal' for carts—there were only five! The Scarinish–Balephetrish length was impassable at the turn of the century and by 1839 many roads were 'worse than a state of nature'. Beaches long formed the best roads on Tiree; the road above Baugh beach dates from around 1910, those above Soroby and Scarinish from 1921 and

1931, and the link across Kilkenneth dunes was made as recently as 1960. Donald Maclean's Breachacha–Arinagour road of 1773 may not have been completed. The northerly end of the present line was cut in the last quarter of the nineteenth century, and the current Coll system was completed in the 1920s by the Gallanach–Sorisdale road. The road 'carried across the Island of Eigg, by . . . statute labour' before 1836 was 'unfinished' eleven years later, and as late as 1881 Rum's only road was the quarter-mile from the pier to Kinloch. Pony-drawn 'sledges' which needed no roads were still being made by the Eigg miller in the 1890s.

The first tarred surface was at Scarinish in 1931. Tarring was in progress when Louis MacNeice visited Coll in 1937 but 'the surface procured is, they told me, no use at all and wears out in a month'. Eigg's main road was tarred in the 1960s, Muck's in the 1970s. Several croft-access roads have been made since the last war; Kenovay to Cornaigbeg, Tiree, was built in 1975, and the one at Cleadale, Eigg, is undoubtedly the best road on Small Isles. A link from Totronald, Coll, to Clabhach would be convenient, and improvement to Rum's austere tracks would not come amiss; schemes for both are in the OPMAC files. Except on Tiree where the RAF did some 'dualling', nearly all roads are single-tracked. Rum and Canna have no public roads; their vehicles are not registered or taxed.

Tiree's first car dates from Edwardian times—a great-niece of Lady Victoria Campbell recalls an old man hiding as it approached. In 1937 MacNeice counted twenty-eight cars at Gott pier to meet *Lochearn*, and twenty on Coll. Eigg's first car arrived in 1921 and there were only two or three until the mid-1960s. The islands' first fatal road accident—but not, alas, their last—occurred on the Arinagour–Breachacha road in 1933.

# THE ISLANDS AT WORK AND PLAY

### AGRICULTURE

HILL farmers breed calves and lambs for sale. An economic hill farm must have land suitable for growing a substantial proportion of the food needed to maintain breeding stock through the winter, a point of particular importance on islands, where imports are costly. Store farmers breed calves and lambs and bring them towards maturity before sale. A store farm must have some rich grazing, and outwintering or winter-keep land for next year's saleable animals as well as for the breeding stock. Rum has little such ground: in 1790 Alexander Maclean was drawing $1\frac{1}{2}$d per acre rent when Clanranald was getting 1s 6d from Eigg. At the other extreme Tiree's sown grass and crops amount to a fifth of its rough pasture.

| | year | Small Isles | Coll | Tiree |
|---|---|---|---|---|
| Beef-cattle | 1961 | 591 | 1,356 | 3,923 |
| ,,      ,, | 1972 | 641 | 1,608 | 4,302 |
| % ( + or − ) | | + 8 | + 18 | + 10 |
| Sheep | 1961 | 6,975 | 9,631 | 12,748 |
| ,, | 1972 | 5,862 | 10,073 | 13,902 |
| % ( + or − ) | | − 16 | + 5 | + 9 |

All cattle were brucellosis-accredited by 1972. Rum carried no cattle or sheep in 1961, and a few Highlanders in 1972.

29 'Town and country': *(above)* the hotel at the head of Scarinish inlet, Tiree *(R. Petrie)*;
30 *(below)* the Eigg main road winds down to the crofting townships of Cuagach and Cleadale *(John Currie)*

31 (above) The rich crofting flats of Ballevulin township, western Tiree (Scotland's Magazine);
32 (below) Ceann a Mhara, southwest Tiree (D. C. Thomson)

| Acres of | year | Eigg, Canna, Muck | Coll | Tiree |
|---|---|---|---|---|
| Rough grazing | 1972 | 8,534 | 15,529 | 15,905 |
| Sown grass | 1961 | 462 | 652 | 3,236 |
| | 1972 | 437 | 577 | 2,889 |
| % ( + or − ) | | − 5 | − 11 | − 11 |
| Oats | 1961 | 79 | 132 | 744 |
| | 1972 | 30 | 97 | 505 |
| Turnips, swedes, | 1961 | 12 | 13 | 16 |
| kale cabbage | 1972 | 5 | 0 | 9 |
| Potatoes | 1961 | 11 | 8 | 80 |
| | 1972 | 6 | 5 | 50 |
| Total crops | 1961 | 110 | 187 | 1,015 |
| | 1972 | 41 | 147 | 588 |
| % ( + or − ) | | − 63 | − 21 | − 42 |

Silage suits the climate better than hay and is commonly made on larger holdings. Roots have declined relative to sown grass which needs no hoeing and is harvested mechanically. Although mechanisation is not an unmixed blessing when spare parts may be days away, horses had largely gone by 1961—428 on Tiree in 1940 were down to 50. Remote Muck saw its first tractor in 1947. Tiree's first 'combine' arrived in 1976.

A good hill herbage depends partly on a low ratio between sheep and total cattle, for the former are selective grazers, leaving many plants to go rank and die. Between 1961 and 1972 Small Isles' ratio fell from 11 to 9, Coll's from 7 to 6, and Tiree's was steady around 3—an indication of their differing conditions. Bracken flourishes when cultivated ground is turned over to sheep, whereas cattle trample down its young shoots; all the islands have bracken trouble. Several panaceas have come and gone; currently Asulox spray seems to have real hope of success.

The Stewarts brought Ayrshire cattle to Coll in the 1850s and Shorthorns came later elsewhere, but Highland blood predominated until World War I. In 1913 the Board of

Agriculture sent fourteen Highland bulls to Tiree and two to Coll, but by 1919 nearly all 'official' bulls were quick-maturing Aberdeen-Angus, not entirely suited to rough and wet conditions. Galloways were popular between the wars; now Herefords, Luings, Blue-Greys and exotic Charrolais and Simenthal are flourishing.

Traces of Soay-type sheep remained on Eigg until recently, but hardy Scottish Blackface (BF) have long been the commonest breed on most islands. Cheviots on BF ewes were probably responsible for the fine reputation once enjoyed by Eigg lamb. On better ground Border Leicesters on BF or Cheviot ewes produce the early-maturing Scottish Half-Bred. Finally the Half-Bred may be crossed with a downland ram.

### Eigg

Eighteen crofts below the Beinn Bhuidhe cliffs are run by a handful of crofters. On paper Cleadale township's 14 each have 2–6 acres arable, 12 grazing and a share in 110 common grazing; Cuagach's 4 have 7–16 acres arable and share 148 common acres. There are no sheep. Fine eighteen-month cattle are raised from the Department's Shorthorn or Aberdeen-Angus bulls, kept in Bull Bay below the coastal cliffs. Hay and roots are the staple winter-keep—heat losses make small-scale ensiling difficult, although it has been tried. Crofters have jobs on the estate, or as postman, ferryman or car-hirer. Much land has gone out of cultivation because drainage is not fully maintained, mechanisation has reduced estate jobs, and youngsters are unwilling to stay in this beautiful back-of-beyond. The rest of the island is farmed by the proprietor's Eigg Estate.

In the 1930s Eigg lost its yearly stock-sale (held on the fields below Sandavore) and had to depend on Oban as it does today. Darling's 1947 *West Highland Survey* painted a gloomy picture of Eigg farming, but the estate had just been let to a tenant who was 'reversing the trend to many sheep and few cattle by keeping . . . 120 Galloway cows'. The

146

Runcimans reverted to factors; John Rutherford did much to make the island more self-sufficient—eg by installing a workshop and sawmill.

In 1964 Robert Evans brought in a lively young hill-farmer and thirty Herefords. The bull and heifers suffered from the rough conditions but their calves thrived. Luing bulls were imported in 1970–1 and the crosses sold well. About 100 calves a year were exported, the aim being to double that number. The sheep were BF hefted to the southern moorland, and South Country Cheviots to the northern plateau, the aim being to export 900 lambs. New ground was broken, the cropping area increased, a ryegrass mixture adopted for sown grass and a grass-dryer installed. Silage was made in Kildonnan barn—the beasts preferred it to hay. The 1926 estate-boat *Dido* brought in fertiliser and concentrates, and ferried lambs to Arisaig, whence an estate lorry took them south. Anglyn Trust, owners from 1972, engaged Angus Mac-Kinnon as farm manager, a crofter of acknowledged skill and experience.

Keith Schellenberg is recovering and draining land long lost (eg the rich Grulins, given over to sheep since 1853) and plans to raise cattle exports to 200 and increase woodland to 300 acres. He has set up a craft workshop at Kildonnan House (formally opened in 1976 by Professor Alexander, chairman of the HIDB), and there is to be a permanent camp site close by. Other possibilities include a knitwear factory, bakery, and even a mini-distillery at Cleadale. Reversing declining population is a formidable task. All—not least the Eigg folk —wish him well.

## Canna

In 1974 John Campbell had 26 pedigree Highland and 26 crossing cows with followers, 500 BF and 500 Cheviot ewes (the hoggs wintered at home). There were 32 acres of rotation grass, 12 of oats, $1\frac{1}{2}$ of early potatoes and 1 of turnips. He employed two shepherds, a tractorman, a boy and a summer student. Four crofters raised cattle on the ten Sanday crofts.

## Muck

Muck is farmed by Lawrence MacEwen. In 1972 it carried 64 cows, 10 heifers and 25 yearling stirks, mostly Galloway/ Shorthorn crosses for crossing with 2 Luing bulls. From 1 January the beasts are indoors for four months and have silage and hill-cow cobs daily. Calving extends from February to May. In summer calves run on the hill with their mothers. Bull-calves are castrated and de-horned, and heifers inoculated against brucellosis. In October calves for sale are separated from their mothers at the pier, roped on the Muck launch and lifted on to MacBrayne's cargo/cattle boat by sling and derrick. That terrifying experience, a possibly stormy passage and lack of milk are not the best preparation for the Oban sales—and there can be no question of bringing them back if prices are low.

In 1972 200 BF and 300 South Country Cheviots were carried. The ewes are out all winter and are dosed against liver-fluke in February. At an early March gathering lean ones are given hill-sheep cobs. Lambing starts around 15 April in enclosed fields; the second lamb of twins is fostered on a ewe who has lost her own (its fleece is used to wrap the twin). Sheep are dipped against tick and maggot-fly, and inoculated.

Lambs are ear-tagged in June and have tails docked for cleanliness; in 1972 around eighty males were selected to be next year's shearlings for sale privately and to the Department of Agriculture—a compliment to Muck's prize-winning sheep. Other male lambs are castrated. Last year's lambs and ewes without lambs are clipped on seasonal rise of the wool; the old people prefer hand-clipping, but electric shears are more often used. Ewes with lambs are sheared at a 'milk-clipping' in mid-July. At the August dipping, lambs are inoculated against clostridial diseases and dosed against worms before being weaned and put into fields already cut for hay or silage.

Cast ewes are drawn out to keep the stock in balance; with wedder and ewe lambs (the 'main crop') they go for finishing to a Border farm run by Lawrence MacEwen's brother. The year's Cheviot ewe lambs (now six months old) are driven over to Horse Island on a low tide, to spend a draughty winter.

Towards the end of November ewes are gathered and again dosed against liver-fluke, and shearling ewes are inoculated. From 20 November to the year-end the stock tups and ewes are put in fenced-off areas. To assess breeding potential, each new ram has a harness containing coloured crayon; when he serves he leaves a mark on the ewe's rump, later given to the lambs she produces. Pregnant ewes winter out: BF on the rough western glens, Cheviots on middle and east hills. On 1 January tup hoggs and the Department's male lambs are brought inside to be hand-fed with bruised oats, hay and chopped turnips.

About 100 acres are fenced-in, nearly all for winter feed. Grass seed contains Italian ryegrass which germinates and grows at soil temperatures 5° less than local natural grasses. Around 1 April part of the grassland is given 2 nitrogen, 1 potash, 1 phosphate (basalt ground is phosphate-deficient). Early in May several fields are shut and fertilised to encourage hay and silage grasses; if the weather is kind they will be ready for cutting by forage harvester in mid-June. Grass for silage goes to a clamp at Gallanach. Hay is also made; three consecutive sunny days make cut grass dry enough to place in the picturesque 5cwt ricks, supported by traditional tripods and topped by waterproof caps, but it may be six weeks before the hay can go to barns. Oats are sown with a fiddle after high-phosphate fertilising in March–April. In May the fields are spread with weedkiller. The crop is cut in August–September by reaper-binder and put into four-sheaved West Highland stooks to be brought to barns and threshed in October. Oats are fed to stock, chaff makes bedding and straw is given to young cattle.

Muck has a small stud of West Highland ponies. Other products usually include 2 acres of potatoes and a few carrots, which do well in the sandy ground and are free from carrot-fly. Rotation is 4 years' grass, 1 year oats, 1 roots and 1 oats undersown with grass. Basic slag is spread every third year and lime is also applied. Machinery is kept off wet ground: good land is the irreplaceable capital asset for continued life on the island. In 1967 a wet summer was followed by 9in of rain in October—the MacEwens finished leading their corn on 14 November. Real skill and determination are needed to farm in such conditions.

## Coll

In 1944–6 Frank Fraser Darling's *Coll Conference* surveyed the island. 'Much of the sandy land, arable and rough grazing . . . shows signs of intensive over-grazing and the damage done by rabbits is quite fantastic. In the north-east . . . conditions are approaching utter dereliction.' Some land was unproductive because the drain from Machair Mor was blocked; it had been obstructed before (see p 55). Lack of phosphates was causing protein deficiency in herbage and low milk-yields. The re-opened cheese factory was uneconomic: a gallon of milk costing 2s produced 1lb of cheese selling at 9d. Although maintenance and improvement expenditure nearly equalled the rent-roll, £60,000 was needed to put the old farms 'into good running order as efficient dairying holdings'. The Conference's principal argument was simple: 'If dairying is the main industry . . . a population of 300–400 can be supported . . . If the island is to be ranched for store cattle, ten or a dozen families will be enough.' The Highlands and Islands Advisory Panel (toothless predecessor to the HIDB) took no notice. Dairying died, and the cheese factory closed around 1956. Coll stockraising is now a success story; but the Conference may yet be right about the population.

Since the Conference, sheep have doubled and beef cattle quadrupled. Ian Mackenzie of Iona grazes 100 cattle at Caoles without winter keep or full-time staff on one of the lowest-cost farms in Scotland. C. K. M. Stewart's farms produce excellent Highlanders, cross Luing/Herefords and dairy

Fresians, and BFs, North Country Cheviots, cross-Leicesters and cross-Suffolks.

In 1964 Coll Properties bought Acha, Kilbride and Arinagour (leased to C. K. M. Stewart), Cliad and Friesland, and Gallanach which they farmed themselves, adding Achamore in 1970. The company is owned by Jan de Vries, physicist and head of Bredero NV Utrecht, a multi-national building, civil engineering and environmental organisation; he lives at the Factor's House, Arinagour, when on the island. Drainage and improvement increased Gallanach's winter keep to 180 acres. Oats were grown as a nurse crop and kale was tried. Most grass is ensiled; storage has now reached 1,800 tons. Rough grazings are fenced into seven hill parks. Shelter-belt planting, although not always successful, is to be continued. In 1968 the stock included 78 cows; by 1972 150 were carried of which 50 were Blue-Greys running with a Hereford bull, the remainder being sired by Luings. The aim was 300 cows producing pedigree Luing calves. A thousand BF ewes (probably the optimum) have four seasons with BF tups, a fifth with Border Leicesters and an experimental sixth with Improvers. Gallanach/Achamore is run by a farm manager, two farmworkers and a shepherd.

*Tiree*

Apart from Scarinish and the factor's farm at Heylipoll, Tiree is almost wholly crofted. In the early 1970s 276 crofts organised in twenty-seven townships were held by 218 crofters. Several crops in one field may give the impression of strip-cultivation but most crofts have had their own fenced arable since the 1930s. Much grazing is still used communally under township committees who determine each croft's *souming*, or stocking-rate. However, several townships have apportioned grazing between individual crofters (administrative help and fencing grants are available from the Crofters Commission); for the crofter this means freedom to change his husbandry at will, but the visitor's freedom to range over the island is gradually being restricted.

Few crofters have less than 10 acres arable and some have much more; most work full-time on their land. Almost all townships extend from the shore—still a source of fertilising shell-sand and seaweed—through rich grazing (*machair*), arable (*achadh*) and rough grazing (*sliabh*). The usual rotation is grain, roots, grain and three years' grass. Grain is commonly rye, and small oats for lighter ground. Late ploughing is dictated by the need to avoid blowing, but the August/early September harvest may still be weeks ahead of the mainland. Most crops go for feed, although many cattle are out-wintered. Barley once grown for both bread and feed has almost gone: 34 acres in 1961, 4 in 1972.

Sales are held at Crossapoll and Scarinish three or four times a year. Annual exports are well over 1,000 cattle and 5,000 sheep. Encouraged by the resident Vet, in spring 1970 the crofters made Tiree the first area in Britain declared free from brucellosis. The warble-fly was eliminated two years later and cattle no longer stand in the sea on summer days to shield their legs from that maddening irritant. Machair improvement is being studied by the West of Scotland Agricultural College; native grasses are supplemented by ryegrass cocksfoot and timothy to lengthen the growing season. Rotavation, high-nitrogen fertiliser, seeding and rolling are being investigated as substitutes for ploughing machair. Manganese is being used on machair soils to promote the growth of large white oats.

At Kenovay 2,000sq ft of glasshouses have produced 3 tons of tomatoes annually but expansion was inhibited by lack of piped water. Daffodil and tulip bulb-growing in open fields, started on Coll and Tiree in 1957, suited the light soils, involved low freight charges and had an assured market; two dozen crofters were planting by 1960. One plot was in the walled garden of the old keepers' cottages at Hynish, but elsewhere protection from the wind was commonly given by fine-mesh wire fences. However, the intensive labour needed, including yearly transplanting to minimise disease, interfered with work on the cattle. A mechanical planter was tried in

1964 but by 1972 total bulbs were down to a quarter-acre. Pigs have long gone. Between 1961–72 dairy cows fell from 377 to 61 and poultry from 3,793 to 1,328.

Tiree has problems of sub-let croftland grazed rather than cropped (when there are still men wanting land), of maintaining fencing with limited labour and no grant, of overstocking and high transport charges; but the island is firmly established as a viable crofting enterprise.

## Rum

In 1797 Edward Daniel Clarke thought Rum offered 'a treasure to the naturalist, which I trust will in future be less neglected'. A century and a half later the Scottish Wild Life Conservation Committee had the same idea: 'It would make an outstanding station for research, and indeed is the most suitable island for this purpose in Scotland.' There were three principal reasons for that categorical statement. The diverse geology and great range of altitudes provide a remarkable variety of soils and vegetation. Rum has been as ruthlessly deforested, overgrazed by sheep, subjected to muirburn and overgrazed by deer as any land in northern Scotland, and is as good a place as any to study how the damage might be repaired. Indeed it is better than most, because access is controllable—which was the third reason. In 1957 the Nature Conservancy bought the island for £23,000 from Sir George's Trustees, and declared it a reserve on the same day as St Kilda.

The experienced grazing tenant, feeling that conservation and farming might not be compatible, took his 53 cattle and 1,700 sheep off. A storm broke over the Conservancy's head. Why choose Rum when there were 610 uninhabited islands? Was the nation not short of food? Another arose when the Conservancy issued a statement declaring themselves 'firm supporters of public access' (giving their St Kilda policy as an example!) yet severely restricting entry. The public would be confined to 500 acres around Scresort; accredited groups of mountaineers might visit the Coolins; 'naturalists and other visitors able to assist in survey or rehabilitation' might have entry permits for scientific purposes. In fact no access trouble has ever arisen, largely owing to the common-sense of Peter Wormell, warden from the outset until 1973.

The Conservancy's primary objects were to restore vege-tation and to develop higher and self-sustaining biological production. Shelter was to be provided and habitats diversified, but flora and fauna were to be conserved. The differing demands of development and conservation required some policy decisions: once-native trees and shrubs should be planted but exotic species introduced only for particular reasons (eg as nurse stock); no sheep or cattle should be introduced; overgrazing by deer should be reduced by culling to around 1,450 and that figure held to give stable conditions during the mapping of vegetation; ponies should be held at 20, sufficient to carry deer carcasses; goats should be reduced from 185 to 25 (easier said than done); areas should be fenced for afforestation.

A series of surveys was launched: of geology, climate, hydrology, soils, soil fauna, vegetation, fungi, vertebrates and insects (over 2,000 species have now been recorded) and of every conceivable aspect of deer behaviour—as well as some that a layman finds it difficult to conceive. Production studies involved sequential cropping, weighing and analysis of plant material from various types of soil and regime. It was found, for instance, that monthly cutting of herb-rich grassland at ground level reduced production, whereas cutting $2\frac{1}{2}$in (6cm) up doubled it. Erosion experiments on Hallival showed that wind action could move stony material yards uphill. Improv-ing acid ground by flushing with streamwater containing lime was tried for three years, with little effect. A fertilised/ unfertilised ground experiment on Hallival produced the unsurprising conclusion that fertilising helped. Twenty-six plots covering various vegetation types were marked-out; unfenced plots revealed the effect of withdrawing sheep, fenced plots the effect of withdrawing all grazing. On unfenced plots growth was greatest on poor soils—deer had taken to eating the better grasslands previously grazed by sheep—but grass tussocks spread. On fenced plots floristic changes were greater on fertile soils. Vegetational recovery was a matter of increased height and density, for the number of species tended to fall.

The Forestry Commission advised that only $2\frac{1}{2}$ per cent of the island was fit for commercial timber, and planting to diversify moorland habitats started in 1958, seedbeds being set up on the Castle lawn. Transplant lines were established in the old walled orchard, where drought-sensitive birch and alder were given overhead irrigation; in 1969–70 60,000 plants a year were produced. The first dozen years saw 200 acres planted—175 were in North Side Enclosure (north of Scresort and Kinloch Glen), the rest being at Kilmory, Papadil, Harris and the Castle. Lodgepole pine and European larch were used for shelter and nurse species. The vegetation survey formed a basis for planting policy:

| plant community on site | tree species planted |
| --- | --- |
| Blanket Bog | Lodgepole pine |
| Wet heath | Scots pine, rowan, whin |
| Calluna heath | Scots pine, rowan, whin, birch |
| Herb-rich heath | Whin, birch, broom, hawthorn, European larch, hazel, oak |
| Molinia grassland | Birch, alder, grey sallow |
| Species-rich grassland | Birch, European larch, hazel, ash, aspen, bird cherry oak |
| Marsh | Alder, grey sallow, ash, aspen |
| Schoenus fen | Alder |

Ground preparation was by single-mouldboard drainage plough. Phosphate and chemical weeding were given after planting.

In April 1969 fire swept North Side Enclosure but its effects were minimised by prompt local action and help from the Eigg brigade—which turned out on smoke signal—and Muck. Early Scots pine were a total loss and other softwoods lost 50 per cent, but most hardwoods recovered by coppicing after being cut to ground-level. Latterly 35 acres a year have been planted in the enclosure.

As the 1970s opened it was no longer necessary to exclude stock in the interests of maintaining a stable range for deer studies, which were nearing completion. In May 1971 Rum's grazing regime was diversified by the introduction of nineteen pure-bred Highland cattle, since developed into a sizeable herd.

### FISHING AND THE SEA

'Herrings frequent the Bay of Gott,' Tiree's minister wrote in 1793, 'yet there are no nets.' In 1846 there were 76 boats —mostly 17-footers with two square sails—but only 19 had tackle! Eviction from the land changed the picture; within a few decades boats were fishing from Heanish, Balemartine, Balephuil, Salum and Milton, and Coll long-liners were landing 100 tons of cod and ling a year. There were few piers and most vessels had to haul-out, which made the trade dangerous; in 1856 a violent north-westerly swept all seven Balephuil boats away to Islay, and nine men died. Tiree smacks, which started by shipping Ayrshire coal when the 8th Duke stopped peat imports, became general Hebridean carriers—thirty were operating before steam took over at the end of the century. Steam drifters working close inshore killed long-line fishing, but a herring trade built up, still worth £2,000 in 1926, only to fade away in the 1930s.

Many Tiresians served in the merchant navy and attained command in MacBraynes and 'deep-sea'. The tradition continues—there were twenty-three merchant seamen on the 1973 Register of Electors.

Over-fishing eliminated lobsters from Muck before 1883 but they seem plentiful enough today, although fished by boats from Eigg and Coll and by several from Tiree (which use Milton pier, reconstructed and given a new access road in 1972, when the catch was valued at £16,000). HIDB give grants and loans for the vessels and their sophisticated navigation equipment: two Tiree craft cost £30,000 apiece in 1975.

Whelks are collected on Eigg, a cold and wet occupation. Scallop-processing was tried on Tiree in 1969. Seaweed is still harvested there for Alginate Industries at Barcaldine.

### THE PROJECT TRUST, BREACHACHA CASTLE

On Coll old Breachacha Castle is in business again. In 1966 Major Nicholas Maclean Bristol, a descendant of the Crossapol Macleans, bought the ruin, persuaded the Secretary of State to waive innumerable byelaws and commenced reconstruction. It was not yet complete when in 1972 he retired from formal army service and moved in with his wife and their small children. One can feel only awestruck admiration for the Hon Lavinia Bristol, who set up home in partially completed rooms where the only natural light is from a couple of gunslits in 7ft thick walls.

Nicholas Bristol is Vice-Chairman of Project Trust, founded in 1967 to organise voluntary work overseas for young people between school and university, and the castle is his headquarters. Over 300 have been placed in locations varying from an Ethiopian blind school to a Patagonian estancia; candidates spend a preliminary period at Breachacha.

The castle was thoroughly researched before reconstruction. The tower has four storeys each of one room 17ft by 13ft accessed by stone spiral stairs: HQ Project Trust is in a garret chamber on the parapeted roof. Curtain walls enclose two sides of the tower, and a building 25ft by 12ft. The castle probably dates from the second quarter of the fifteenth century (when John Garbh established the Colls as a separate clan?) and may be contemporary with Kisimul Barra. During Duart/Coll feuds in the sixteenth century the parapet and curtain were raised—firearms were then in use—and remnants of an outside artillery stance are associated with seventeeth-century defence against Campbells. After the 1679 surrender the internal building, formerly a hall, was converted into a three-storey dwelling. The loyal Hector abandoned the castle in 1750 when he moved into his adjacent mansion.

In one respect Breachacha was surely unique among castles —it had no internal water supply. That unlikely fact, its *bijou* size, its vulnerable site on a gentle flower-decked shore, and its contemporary roles of comfortable home and international head-office, make it a building of dreams. One of the Bristol boys sleeps in 'John Garbh's bed' formed in the thickness of a tower wall—this is the enviable world of *Treasure Island*.

### ISLAND OCCUPATIONS

Coll recently saw another valiant and successful enterprise. In 1966 Ronnie and Mairi Hedderwick set up the Malin Workshop at Crossapoll based on her talent for drawing and his miraculous ability to run a printing works with no road access; but expanding business and the difficulty of secondary education caused them to transfer to Fort William in 1974.

Ian Christie's Hebridean Knitwear Factory, established in the FC church at Kirkapoll, Tiree, in 1971, employs nineteen girls, and the staff will double when new premises are completed. The Rum folk make craftwork from shells, semi-precious stones, deerskins and goatskins and craft enterprises have recently been started on Eigg, Muck and Tiree.

Another occupation loomed in 1961 when the Home Secretary considered using small islands for the confinement of prisoners; in 1966 Lord Mountbatten's Committee of Inquiry into prisons thought 'Muck Isle' might be suitable. Fortunately the 'problem' of providing 'reasonable living conditions' caused the idea to be dropped.

### THE ISLANDS IN WARTIME

Memories of World War I are dim; a few mines came ashore: one at Scarinish, Tiree, another at Grulins, Eigg, said to have exploded when the minister threw stones at it! In July 1918 a submarine shelled the mailboat *Plover* on passage from Tiree to Castlebay. Two boats were lowered: the mate's landed at Harris, Rum, and its occupants reputedly walked to Kinloch 'in their bare feet'; and the captain's made Castlebay at dawn—to find *Plover* tied up at the pier. Her remaining crew had fired at the sub (which sheared off) and resumed course—with a Tiree man at the wheel.

In 1940, when Atlantic convoys were re-routed north-about Ireland, Hebridean airfields became an urgent requirement. Tiree's civil grass-strip was requisitioned in August; contractors imported hordes of unruly labourers, and in November 1941 RAF Reef was ready for service. Operational aircraft did not arrive until 8 April 1942, when Coastal Command brought in Hudsons of 224 Squadron; they flew their first convoy-escort six days later. No 304 Polish Squadron flew Wellingtons in May–June; and 224 Squadron was re-equipped with Wellingtons and Liberators, but left in September. The airfield then went over to 'care and maintenance'. From September 1943, for two years, 518 Squadron trained meteorological reconnaissance crews in Halifaxes, and for a year from February 1944 281 Squadron's Warwicks flew 'live' weather sorties—dangerous work, for aircraft had to go out regardless of flying conditions. No 31 Embarkation Unit, at Scarinish since 1941, disbanded on 31 December 1945, and on 1 July 1946 Reef was transferred to the Ministry of Civil Aviation. The island was left littered with derelict buildings.

Meanwhile life on Tiree had been transformed. Island House was requisitioned. Gun emplacements sprang up alongside ancient hill forts. A hutted town lined the road from Heanish to Crossapol, where the WAAF quarters and the NAAFI canteen—Tiree's first licensed premises—were equal centres of interest. RAF lads in billets were virtually 'adopted'. RAF trucks brought island lasses to dances in Crossapol Hall, and Tiresians in general to the camp theatre where many saw their first live show and heard their first concert. As an old cottager put it thirty years later: 'We had some fun in those days'.

The war's dark side is recalled by memorials on Tiree and Coll. Several ships came ashore and many were sunk in the seas around, for the Russian and slow-Atlantic convoys passed west of Tiree and Canna, guided by the half-shaded lights at Skerryvore and Heiskeir. There are twenty-three war graves at Soroby, Tiree. The fearful havoc when *Queen Mary* sliced through her escort HMS *Curacao* in October 1942 is commemorated by two graves on Eigg, and two on Muck flanked by those of German submariners.

Yet memories now are of happier things. Of the 6,000-tonner *Nevada II* grounded in July 1942 off north-west Coll, cut down to scrap, loaded into puffers at Sorisdale Bay (her general cargo, including whisky and a reputed million cigarettes, was disposed of more locally). Of the army's first night-exercise on Eigg, when an alarmed islander returned to Muck, uncertain whether the troops were friend or foe. Of Muck's emergency food supply: 1cwt of sugar delivered by a solicitous government at the beginning of the war—and sent for at the end! And of General Stewart commanding the Coll Home Guard as a seventy-six-year-old lieutenant.

### ADMINISTRATION

Small Isles are in Inverness constituency represented by the Liberal Russell Johnson, who startled the European parliament by making his maiden speech in English, French and Gaelic, wearing the kilt. Coll and Tiree are in Argyll, Conservative-held for fifty years until 1974 when it was captured by Scottish Nationalist Iain MacCormick, son of the party's founder. Both MPs probably give the islands more than average attention although, like local councillors, they receive no allowance for travelling about their scattered constituencies.

Island ballot-boxes occasionally make a paragraph in the national press. Small Isles' box goes by police-car from Inverness to Mallaig and thence by service steamer, returning by motor-boat. Eigg school is the only polling-station; a stormy day can disenfranchise Rum, Canna or Muck folk who have not voted by post. From 1970 the Coll and Tiree boxes have been returned by air, and Argyll is no longer the last constituency to declare results.

Originally Eigg was in Inverness-shire and the other islands in Argyll. In 1891 all Small Isles came under Inverness. Until 1975 Small Isles sent one councillor to Lochaber District Council at Fort William and one to Inverness County Council. Now Small Isles/Mallaig/Arisaig share a councillor on Lochaber DC, a second-tier authority in Highland Region. Coll and Tiree formerly had their own DC and returned a councillor jointly to Argyll County. Under reorganisation they return one to Argyll DC at Lochgilphead. With an electorate of 26,000, all Argyll returns only three members to Strathclyde Region, which has an electorate of 1·8 million, and meets in Glasgow.

Some islanders favoured joining Western Isles Region (electorate 23,000) with headquarters at Stornoway, Lewis, feeling that island problems would be better understood there. Others thought communications with Stornoway too difficult, and that Argyll county should be retained or enlarged. No official notice was taken of either view.

## PUBLIC SERVICES

Small Isles have no public water supply. Eigg has only the odd house without piped water, but its small catchments are surprisingly vulnerable to drought. Canna and Sanday are supplied by the estate. Rum's main source is Sir George's reservoir on Coire Dubh burn. Much of Coll depends on local wells. Arinagour was served from the Dairy Loch by General Stewart's scheme until 1958, when Argyll CC provided a reservoir at Loch Airidh aon Oidche; no treatment is needed. Tiree formerly had local wells—one oddly placed on top of Balephetrish Hill. The RAF provided a

K

supply from Loch a Phuill during World War II, which Argyll CC used as a basis for the present scheme. After micro-straining, chlorination and pH correction, loch water is pumped to a reservoir on Ben Hynish and piped throughout the south of the island from Greenhill to Scarinish. Resources could be doubled by using Loch Bhasapoll, and a current project will complete piped supplies to the whole of Tiree by 1981.

Coal is brought annually by puffers and communally unloaded, occasionally across beaches, as at Caoles, Tiree. Bottled gas is much used for lighting and cooking. The Lodge and adjacent houses on Eigg have been served by a DC hydro scheme since the late 1920s, with reservoir in the Lodge grounds and diminutive turbine-house by the Harbour shore. Sir George's hydro plant, latterly supplemented by a diesel set, still supplies electricity on Rum where each house can run an iron, or other small appliance. Several Small Isles' houses have diesel 'Startomatics', which have done much to bring island life into step with modern times. The Hydro Board have schemes (presumably diesel) to give Small Isles public supplies, but seem unlikely to implement them. The RAF built a diesel power station at Tiree airfield and the Board have since doubled its capacity; it employs six men. Distribution covered the island by 1960. Loads are balanced by night-heating, and night-pumping from Loch a Phuill. A scheme to supply Coll by submarine cable across Gunna Sound was completed in 1975; until then a few wind generators dating back to the 1930s supplemented the 'Starto-matics'.

Small Isles have no policemen. Tiree has two and a fine new police house at Scarinish complete with cell. Coll and Eigg have special constables. Eigg has a leading fireman and six other volunteers, whose portable pump lives at the pier. Rum has Sir George's hydrant main, a portable pump, forest fire-fighting stations, fire-breaks and 'early warning' arrange-ments with MacBraynes, neighbouring islands and the main-land. Coll has a volunteer party with a pump at Arinagour.

Tiree has a retained fireman, volunteer parties with pumps at Scarinish and Cornaigmore, and a fire-point at Balemartine; cover is also given by Reef airport. Fire is a menace in these isolated places, and it seems a pity that the authorities do not follow Nature Conservancy's example and give an extinguisher to every household—a more practical step than the 'flying firemen' currently envisaged.

Rubbish is a growing problem. Tiree has had a collection to tip since the mid-1960s, and one is now planned for Coll. On Rum each house has a dustbin—the contents go to sea. Soon after the Conservancy took over it collected huge quantities of scrap metal; similar operations seem desirable elsewhere, for the number of abandoned cars grows yearly.

### HOUSING

Island building is expensive. 'I do not understand,' the 5th Duke wrote to his Tiree factor in 1803, 'how it should happen that Morison asks £166 for building a school-house like those which only cost £50 in Kintyre.' The sentiment remains relevant today. A handsome prefab house was built on Eigg in the early 1970s. Another prefab was brought to Canna in 1971—on lorries via the new pier-slipway. The Conservancy has built two houses on Rum and has re-vamped the White House (which dates from 1880), the warden's house and office. Since 1955 Argyll County has provided 12 council houses at Arinagour, Coll, and 42 on Tiree, where 16 more are currently planned at Crossapoll. Many good older houses, now 'second homes', lie empty for much of the year.

Tiree's old cottages are highly functional. Shortage of stone caused their walls to be sand-filled; total thickness often exceeds 5ft, and window openings are like tunnels. Shortage of timber caused the light collar-tied rafters to span between inner leaves, leaving a broad exposed wallhead. High winds caused rafter-ends to be built well into walls (which restricted headroom), and thatch had to be held down by cattle knee-bones, sheep-ribs and a plait of weighted ropes. Wallheads formerly grew flowers and were grazed by sheep and even cattle. Now they are cemented and less picturesque—but the walls are dry. In the absence of barley and rye, thatch is currently made of bents, often held down by chicken wire; but most cottage roofs are close-boarded, tarred and felted. Tiree's peat shortage led to early abandonment of central fires—and to 'the very superior cleanliness of the persons and homes of the inhabitants . . . [whose] skin and clothes and belongings do not become stained with peat smoke as in the other islands'.

### SHOPS AND SOCIAL LIFE

Freight charges and low turnover increase prices; in 1974 a basket of goods costing £7.22 in Edinburgh was priced at £8.67 in Tiree.

Tiree has a bank (since 1949), Co-op store, grocers, butcher, baker (since 1972), electrical shop, repair garage and building contractor. The Council of Social Service has groups dealing with agriculture, water, welfare, tourism and transport; a PO minibus service started in 1975. There is a National Farmers' Union branch with 100 members. The Agricultural Society runs an annual show. The yacht club has a two-day regatta and shows films. The Glasgow Tiree Association has held annual sports on the island for seventy-six years. There are meals-on-wheels, home helps, adult education and Gaelic classes, a branch of An Comunn Gaidhealach, a uniformed pipe band, a golf club with a nine-hole course at Vaul, football and badminton clubs, a fifty-member youth club, Baptist Youth Fellowship, Guides and Brownies. The ageing public hall at Crossapoll, where there are commonly two dances a week to the music of the island dance band, cannot cope with all this activity, which spills over into church and school halls. Social work includes fostering children boarded out from Glasgow, started in 1906. At the end of World War II numbers had reached 120, but policy changes reduced demand and in the early 1970s ten foster parents were caring for thirty-eight children.

Arinagour, Coll, has two shops, a launderette, and a hall built in 1953. There is a troupe of Highland dancers. The Coll Agricultural and Horticultural Society held its 54th Annual Show in 1975. The Glasgow Coll Association dates from 1931. There is a Community Committee, a Women's Guild, and home-help service. In the 1950s the Stewart car took Collachs to church by trailer; the complete absence of public transport can be a handicap.

Eigg has occasional—and highly successful—garden fêtes supported by both churches, and inter-Small Isles sports days. There are country-dancing, discussion, craftware and knitting groups. Dances are held at the hall in the Lodge grounds, and the new proprietor has introduced exotic sports such as rugby. As on other islands, mail-order firms are well patronised; for more immediate wants there is a well-stocked shop (run by the Co-op until 1967) with a beer licence.

Rum's post office/shop has a spirits licence. The community shows films in its fine hall and is currently building a swimming-pool. Much of the money for both was raised on the island's open days, when special boats have brought large numbers of people to walk nature trails, tour the castle, ride Rum ponies, buy local craftwork and view an exhibition of Conservancy projects.

The Canna men enjoy billiards at Canna House. There is a post office but no shop; goods come out from Mallaig. The great hayshed at Gallanach, Muck, has seen some memorable dances. Catriona and Alastair MacEwen were married from there in 1968–9. For shopping and post the island relies on Eigg.

Radio and TV have not closed the islands' ever-open doors. A 'wee crack' over a dram or a coffee still accompanies the briefest call. Conversation is an art not yet lost.

## TOURISM

'Far off in summers I shall not see,' wrote the 8th Duke, 'the island of Tiree will be a great resort of health.'

In the early nineteenth century each inland had its inn, and there were numerous pubs. The Rum and Muck inns closed before the 1826–8 emigrations, Canna's when MacNeill took over, and Tiree's when the 8th Duke succeeded. Coll Hotel, established by 1856, was giving a 'warm and cheery welcome' ten years later (it is unlikely to have been Boswell's 'little poor public house close up on the shore'). The Duke set up Scarinish Hotel around 1870 (it may be the Inn existing in 1801). Donald Macleod's Scoor Hotel, Eigg (now Galmisdale House) was opened by the 1870s. An 1894 guest at the Scarinish reported 'a kindly landlady, a quiet sitting-room and a clean bedroom', but tea, tinned meat and Glasgow bread and jam appeared at every meal. It was many years before all island landladies grasped that their visitors actually *liked* porridge, scones and barley bread, and that mackerel, lythe and saithe could tempt human palates, as well as lobsters into creels. Visitors now come from all sections of society, but the islands were once playgrounds of the middle classes, attracting a due proportion of eccentrics. An Eigg diarist wrote in 1913: 'Met a party of 10 from the inn, disporting themselves on the sands, one playing the pipes and the others—even the stoutest—hopping in single file after him. This is Mrs Kennedy-Fraser's party.' That formidable lady was presumably collecting material for the second edition of *Songs of the Hebrides*, which she published in 1922 jointly with Eigg's Rev Kenneth Macleod. The 'inn' was probably Laig Farm, a guesthouse from around 1896 when Thomson closed the Scoor Hotel.

Coll and Tiree's tourism increased rapidly in the 1930s. The new *Lochearn* was comfortable and reliable; there was a fashion for 'fresh-air' holidays, and golfers were amply served by a 'professional' course at Vaul, eighteen holes (marked by tin cans on sticks) on the Reef and nine of the eighteen laid out at Scarinish during the Crofters' War; Coll had nine holes at Breachacha. An excellent 135-page guidebook appeared in 1937. The Coll author was Hector Mac-Dougall, born and bred at delectable but long-deserted

Eileraig, a Glasgow policeman and later a journalist; the Tiree pages were by Rev Hector Cameron, parish minister and author of a book on Tiree bards.

Coll and Tiree are 12 miles from end to end; bicycles are on hire but head winds prevail, and many visitors bring cars. *Claymore* took only six and when trade built up during the 1960s summer Saturdays saw many cars diverted to *Loch Carron*, the cargo boat; her elastic schedule resulted in some anxious vigils on Gott pier late into Saturday night—not the best of ways to start a holiday. Eigg, Muck, the 'open' part of Rum, and Canna are small enough to be covered on foot; getting a vehicle to all but the latter involves planks, ropes and tidal calculations. Parking at Mallaig is none too easy, so many visitors travel north by sleeper from Euston. Breakfast as the train skirts Lomond and climbs to Rannoch Moor, and coffee in the glorious country between Fort William and Mallaig form a memorable opening to any holiday.

The islands have more potential visitors than accommodation. Caravans have not been allowed to proliferate, although several are dotted about Coll's sandhill country; the first came to Eigg in 1965 on an idyllic site above Laig beach. Current accommodation includes:

| | |
|---|---|
| Eigg | 3 guesthouses, a few caravans, cottages to let |
| Canna | 1 cottage giving boarding accommodation |
| Muck | 3 cottages to let (and a guesthouse building) |
| Coll | Coll Hotel (licensed), guesthouses, caravans, cottages to let |
| Tiree | Scarinish Hotel (licensed since 1952), The Lodge Hotel (licensed), guesthouses, a few caravans, cottages to let |

The Conservancy's chief warden should be contacted regarding the restricted accommodation on Rum. The Lochaber and District Tourist Organisation, Cameron Square, Fort William, will help with Small Isles' addresses; the Oban, Mull and District Tourist Organisation, Albany Street, Oban, deals with Coll and Tiree. On Eigg and Muck, guidebooks are published by Lawrence MacEwen; on Coll by Betty Mac-

Dougall (daughter of the author of the 1937 book and President of the Coll Association); and on Tiree by Mona Maclean.

Day-trips to Eigg and Rum run from Arisaig Hotel and Mallaig; trippers are catered for by the bright tearoom on Eigg pier established by the Anglyn Trust and Joan Jameson.

# 13 RELIGION, EDUCATION AND HEALTH

## CHURCHES

FOURTEEN pre-Reformation chapels are recorded in the Tiree parishes of Kirkapoll and Soroby. A papal document of 1373 refers to 'Ayg MacPetri perpetual vicar of the ecclesiastical parish of St Columba Kirkapoll', but in 1421 Soroby was reduced to a chaplaincy. There were ten chapels on Coll and a perpetual (full-time) vicar; in 1433 he was Fyngonius Fyngonii, illegitimate grandson of an abbot of Iona, appointed by family influence but removed when he was found to be unordained and not even a priest! He was perhaps related to the Fingonius Prior commemorated by a well-preserved sculptured stone dated 1414 in the graveyard at An Cladh Beag, the larger of the roofless chapels at Kirkapoll.

The 1560 Reformation resulted from such scandals and from lay envy of church wealth; in 1549 the Bishop of the Isles held Canna and Muck and pocketed the income from Kirkapoll and Soroby.

Immediately before the Reformation Eigg had a 'Paroch kirk'; Canna was served by St Columba's; the Coll church was either Cill Ionagh beyond Gallanach (foundations exist in the graveyard) or Crossapoll (removed by the sea in the nineteenth century), and Tiree had Kirkapoll and Soroby. After 1560, when parliament dismantled the Roman Church in Scotland and made the celebration of mass ultimately punishable by death, priests were banished; it was many years before the first island ministers came to replace them.

*Post-Reformation*

Coll and Tiree's first effective minister was Farquhar Fraser, admitted in 1633 and resident from 1642. He was debarred for having been Maclean of Duart's regimental chaplain on the losing side in the 1645 Civil War and Duart was excommunicated. He confessed to the Synod of Argyll that he preached 'to Sir Lachlan mc Claine, being excommunicat, in his paroach kirk at Tirie, but did desyre Sir Lachlan not to remain in the church in tyme of prayer . . . Sir Lachlan obeyed for two Sabbaths, but would not remove the 3rd'.

Farquhar died in 1678 and was succeeded by his son John, who transferred to Coll and ran into trouble when strict Presbyterianism returned after the 1688 Revolution (see p 62). Although dismissed, he continued 'discharging ministerial duties and subsisting on the . . . benevolence of the parishioners' until his death in 1702. Traditionally he converted two dozen Coll families to Protestantism.

There are numerous tales of the Coll Macleans' forcible conversions. One at least is authentic—General Assembly, Edinburgh, 10 May 1726: 'Hector Maclean of Coll . . . was pleased himself to go with a Protestant Minister to the Isle of Roum, and by God's blessing they have brought over the inhabitants . . .'

The first minister to serve Small Isles (from Sleat) was Neil MacKinnon, admitted around 1620. In 1625 Irish Franciscans from Louvain mounted secret missions in the West and Father Cornelius Ward landed on Eigg. The church was roofless and the people had forgotten the ritual of the mass; Ward baptised sixteen and converted 198. MacKinnon led a night raid 'with soldiers' against his rival but was thoroughly defeated. Ward converted seventeen on Rum and from 14 October was on Canna where the people 'paid more attention to the harvest than to their souls'—very sensibly, considering the date. They told him that when Columba freed Rum of 'all poisonous things' a toad swam to Canna and was turned into a stone. He saw the very stone —it *had* 'the likeness of a toad'. In 1630 Father Patrick Hegerty was on Muck and Eigg. A Lazarist, Father Dermot Dugan, worked in the Hebrides from 1651 and converted '800 or 900' on Eigg, Canna and elsewhere: 'scarce 15 . . . knew any of the mysteries of our holy Faith . . . persons of 70, 80, 100 or even 120 years of age . . . had never received holy baptism'.

*Eighteenth Century*

Under the Patronage Act 1712 landlords virtually appointed ministers, but because the Clanranalds were Catholic the Crown selected those for Small Isles—a separate parish from 1727. The Presbyterian church became landlord-dominated and ministers set up as gentlemen—Tiree's farmed Balephetrish, and the Eigg glebe is said to have been the largest in Scotland. Yet Kirk Sessions, controlled by lay elders, maintained theocratic notions current at the Reformation. They relieved the (deserving) poor; Coll in 1732: 'Ballohodh . . . after prayer. The Session Appoints their Collecter to give John McNeill one shill. being a poor blind boy . . . out of the former fines'. They settled disputes. In 1809 Catherine MacKinnon of Vaul, Tiree, charged Anne MacKinnon with 'taking the substance' from dye; Catherine's husband dismissed such things as 'women's trifles', but had lost milk 'in the same manner'. Anne counter-charged one Widow MacPhail with uttering curses—that she 'might be without a son' and that her calf Sleud Bhreachd might die (it did). The Session fined Catherine for slander, the widow for 'Incantations' and ordered both to be rebuked three Sabbaths before the congregation.

But the vast majority of Session time was spent on sexual matters:

> Cornaigmore 18th April 1787 Margaret Campbell confesses . . . Archibald MacPhail in Cornaigmore had come into her home, and she asleep with her two children. That he asked her for a mutchkin of whiskey . . . That he had gone to bed

with her but remained there so short a time she hardly thought he could be the Father of a Child . . . she thought the matter so trifling . . . He went off without the whiskey . . .

These prurient Gestapos could disgrace—at Heylipoll in 1775 Lachlan Maclean Kenovay, found guilty of calling John Maclean Balephetrish 'the son of a Whore and Bitch', was ordered 'for three successive Sundays to acknowledge the Lie with hanging Lip & stretched out Tongue'. They could fine, but had little ability to enforce payment. Their effective sanction was to refer offenders to the factor—at Scarinish in 1803 the 'scandalous and disorderly conduct' of John McLarty Caoles was 'represented in a Petition to Malcolm McLaurinn Esqr. Chamberlain of Tiry' who ordered John to 'leave the Country'. They were also intolerant, a trait still in fashion with some proprietors; when, in 1770, Eigg's Catholic priest landed on Muck he was 'arrested' and sent packing by the laird's wife.

Two centuries after the Reformation, the Presbyterians started to provide island churches. The Georgian parish church at Gott, Tiree, is said to date from 1776; about that time there were churches built by the 5th Duke at Drimbui and Scarinish (now the old pier store-house). The Duke built a manse at Gott in the 1790s, replaced by a larger one in 1832 (there is now a modern house). Eigg manse dates from 1790 and was enlarged in 1889. Alexander Maclean of Coll built a church and manse at Clabhach in 1802.

*Nineteenth-century events*

Around 1819 an Inverness society sent Small Isles ninety-two Gaelic Bibles and 105 New Testaments. Father Anthony MacDonald of Eigg: 'a wonderful change . . . formerly [the people] devoted the Sabbath entirely to idle conversation or frivolous amusements . . . now they regularly : . . read the Scriptures . . . in many instances the parents are instructed by the children'.

Harmony between Eigg's Catholics and Protestants was cultivated by the Rev Donald Maclean, Small Isles' minister from 1818. Son of a factor of Rum and Muck, he farmed the glebe, Sandavore and Castle Island, married a sister of Dr Maclean, the clearer of Rum, and was a deputy lieutenant of Inverness-shire. In 1834 this pillar of the Establishment was charged with multiple adultery, attempted rape, indecent exposure, assault, giving an oath 'regarding some woman' before his Catholic colleague, drunkenness on foot and horseback, and neglect of duty. On 9 September the Skye Presbytery, acting as prosecutor, judge and jury, heard the case at the Inn of Eigg (now the outbuilding of Galmisdale House); but an unseemly racket from the adjacent beer tent made them move to the school—the present schoolhouse.

The lurid evidence—eg of two young ladies in bed with the minister—covered only a few of the charges, but the case dragged on until 1838 when Maclean wandered drunk into the General Assembly, due to hear one of his numerous appeals. He was deposed and died in the following year. His boon companion in the Harbour pub was Allan MacDonald of Laig, a brawny Catholic tippler (who one dark night, according to tradition, met the Devil on the road back home, recognised him when he felt two horns, threw him over his shoulder and found next morning he had killed his bull). The minister was certainly a heavy drinker, but he may have been the vicarious victim of resentment arising from the Rum and Muck clearances.

His successor, John Swanson who published much nonsense about the Harlot of Rome, brought out some Eigg folk and all those on Rum at the Disruption of 1843, left the manse to live on his yacht *Betsey*, and held fervent meetings in a thatched hut —vestiges of which may still be seen just south of Eigg Manse Bridge. He refused Dr MacPherson's offer of a cottage opposite the present shop, used by later Free Church ministers.

There were Baptists on Tiree in 1820. Twelve years later the Rev Archibald Farquarson, who also served Coll, formed an 'Independent Congregation' at Ruaig (attended by 200 people) and Drimbui (400), and by 1836 Tiree had resident 'United Secessionist' and Baptist ministers. At the Disruption the Rev Archibald Nicol brought out nearly all his Collachs, who met in houses or in the open at Clabhach until, twenty years later, they were granted a site for a church at Grishipoll. Few Tiresians came out.

## Island parishes

Tiree's church organisations grew as the population shrank. A Baptist revival in the 1860s, based on Heanish and Balemartine, later embraced the Congregational church at Cornaigmore. Between 1865 and 1875 Coll, Kirkapoll and Soroby became separate Presbyterian parishes, and Heylipoll Manse was built. In 1876 Tiree became a separate Free Church charge; Kirkapoll church (the knitwear factory) dates from 1880, Scarinish Manse (the Old People's Home) from 1884, and Balinoe church from 1888. A Presbyterian church opened at Cornaigmore in 1899 and Heylipoll parish church, 'a replica of Iona cathedral' was completed in 1904 ('a beautiful edifice—the only building on Tiree to which that epithet applies', according to the 1937 guidebook). The Coll Free Church transferred from Grishipoll to its present building at Arinagour in 1884 and the parish church followed in 1907 (both former churches are now farm buildings). The United Frees built a church at Arinagour around 1900.

By contrast Eigg's first proper church of any denomination (the present building) was opened in 1862; the Rum folk met in a thatched hut throughout the nineteenth century; Canna's round-towered Presbyterian church (in memory of Robert Thom) dates from 1914, and Muck has had no church in recorded times. In 1932 the Archibald MacVicar bequest gave the income from £831 to help provide transport for Small Isles' minister between Eigg, Rum and Canna; oddly, Muck was not included.

The Free Church ministers left Small Isles and Tiree in the 1930s. In 1950 it became 'desirable' instead of 'essential' for the Small Isles' minister to speak Gaelic; in 1973 a corresponding change was made in Coll and Tiree which had been combined into a single parish in 1972. In 1970 Small

Isles became a mission station of Mallaig. Tiree retains a resident minister, Small Isles a resident missionary.

*Roman Catholics*

Most Clanranald MacDonalds were Catholics until Young Clanranald's death in 1777 and most Eigg and Canna folk retained the old faith. Around 1685–1700 each island had a priest, but there seems to have been a gap until 1770 when active proscription ceased. Thereafter Eigg had a priest more-or-less continuously. Apart from the Laigs (1770–1853), the Kildonnan Macleans (1850s–66) and possibly Donald MacNeill, Canna (1848–81), few if any of the principal tenants were Catholics, and the parish was always poor; in 1836 when Donald Maclean's stipend was £150, two Catholic priests shared £20.

The elder was Father Anthony MacDonald, educated at Samalaman, who was on Eigg from 1794 until his death in 1843. Initially he officiated from a Kildonnan croft house, but from 1810 shared premises at Cleadale with a Catholic family, an arrangement not to the liking of his assistant, Father Donald MacKay: 'the underflat . . . for the congregation is entirely unfit for celebrating the most tremendous mysteries of our religion. During divine service I am constantly distracted by pigs, hens etc'. Father Anthony is buried in old St Donnan's chapel at Kildonnan and his saintly memory lives in Eigg tradition.

In 1910 a proper church and priest's house were built on the site of the old Cleadale building. It was adorned by a painting attributed to Zurburan given by Robert Thomson, but damp caused deterioration and in 1957, with the congregation's approval, Sir Steven Runciman had the painting cleaned by the National Gallery. Since then it has been on loan to Oban cathedral.

The striking Catholic church on Sanday built in the 1890s by the 3rd Marquess of Bute is inconveniently situated, and the older chapel of St Columba on the Canna side of the harbour is back in service.

The last resident priest left Eigg in 1952. Eigg is now served from Glenfinnan, and Canna from Knoydart. Visiting priests hold occasional services. Father Barrett-Lennard of Brompton Oratory, a visitor for twenty years, recalls a procession on the evening of 15 August 1958, the Feast of the Assumption: three dozen people took part, chanting plainsong and led by a piper. As they left Laig Beach to cross to the chapel field the sun was setting over Rum and the moon rose over the Sgurr . . .

### SCHOOLS

A single parish school—all that the law required of landlords —was established on Tiree around 1780, and five years later the Scottish Society for the Propagation of Christian Knowledge set up a second. Attendances rose from twenty to 150 after the concession of free places in 1791. These schools were at Drimbui and Kenovay (later Scarinish) until 1804 when the 5th Duke built costly new premises at Heylipoll and Kirkapoll (possibly the Lodge Hotel). Fees were 2 shillings a quarter for reading, 2s 6d for arithmetic, 3s for Latin and 4s for music: 'those who are considered poor should apply to the Factor and Minister and upon their recommendation be taught Gratis'. Eigg parish school replaced an SSPCK 'ambulatory' arrangement in 1793. All schools taught in English, a grievous handicap when 'the language principally spoken and universally understood' was Gaelic. During the nineteenth century, voluntary societies provided a few schools where teaching was in Gaelic.

By 1836 there were nine schools on Tiree (including two parochials, a General Assembly's at Cornaigmore and a Gaelic at Sandaig) and three on Coll (GA's SSPCK's and a Gaelic). The parochial on Eigg was the present schoolhouse built in 1829, and Muck had a Gaelic 'itinerating' teacher. The Free Church Ladies' Association later sent a teacher to Catholic Canna, but MacNeill refused permanent premises.

Sheriff Nicolson's 1865 survey showed 37 per cent of Tiree's children attending eight schools, 17 per cent of young

Collachs at Acha (the only school) and 12 per cent of Small Isles' children at Eigg parochial. No education was provided on Rum, Canna and Muck. Kirkapoll parish school was 'one of the best in the Hebrides', and Nicolson also had kind words for Caoles and Balemartine FC Ladies' schools, which taught in Gaelic, and for Acha 'efficiently run by a certificated master'. Of Tiresian adults 66 per cent could read and 48 per cent could write English or Gaelic; for Eigg the figures were 54 per cent and 34 per cent. Clearly there must have been adult education; one Collach is said to have attended with his grandchildren.

Schools proliferated as populations declined. Arnabost, Coll, opened in 1871. After the 1872 Act made primary education compulsory for all children who could not read and write English, 'side-schools' were provided at the Muck pierhouse, on Sanday and at Kinloch, Rum. Ultimately there was even one at Glen Harris, Rum; the teacher spent alternate weeks with the shepherd's children at Guirdil (approached by a mountain path often impassable on Monday mornings). Tiree's Cornaigmore opened in 1876; the present Eigg schoolroom in the following year. In 1892–9 Arinagour and Cornaig, Coll, replaced Arnabost and the FC Ladies' establishment at Bousd, where the master 'used to march his pupils down to Bosta Strand and teach them their ABC . . . on the smooth sand'.

The wrong-headed insistence on teaching in a foreign language took its toll. A visitor to Eigg school in 1862 noted 'this double-tongued teaching is very uphill work', and in the folowing year 'a few—very few—could do plain English into Gaelic'. Acha school log, 17 January 1871: 'Object lesson given on colour to the whole school. Many of the younger children not understanding owing to their deficiency in the English language and causing me to translate many of the sentences into Gaelic.'

A long-term result was observed by the Irish poet, Louis MacNeice, on Coll and Tiree in 1937: 'The older folk pick their way uncomfortably through English . . . without much

L

expression. But [they] speak Gaelic . . . with fire, speed and dramatic variety.'

The Harris teacher tramped to Guirdil for the last time in 1919, and Harris school closed when that tiny community dispersed in 1926. Muck received its present school in the previous year. By 1937 pupils of Eigg, Rum, Canna and Muck were down to 19, 5, 3 and 3; Coll's schools were at Arinagour, Acha, Grishipoll and Cornaig, Tiree's at Cornaigmore (rebuilt in 1936), Heylipoll, Balemartine, Scarinish and Ruaig. In the 1940s school meals came to Tiree, Coll and Eigg; and Eigg's school transport, which significantly increased winter attendance, pointed a way to concentration elsewhere. A fine new school opened at Arinagour in 1956 with a roll of twenty-two, replacing the four older buildings, and from 1975 school buses brought all Tiree pupils to an extended thirteen-teacher Cornaigmore.

Only Tiree has a 'catchment' large enough to justify local provision of the specialist teaching and expensive equipment needed even for four-year secondary level. Children from the other islands leave home at the age of twelve: Coll's go to Oban; Small Isles' once went to Portree or Mallaig and now go to Fort William. Free hostel accommodation is provided, but children get home only for school holidays. Many parents have left the islands, unwilling to see their families split up. Secondary education has become a potent source of depopulation, and if numbers continue to decline a question-mark must hang over Cornaigmore's excellent but costly secondary department; the total school roll is less than 130.

Muck school closed from 1941 to 1947, when Lawrence MacEwen and his brother Alastair entered; and Canna closed for several years in the 1950s. Intermittency has also threatened Eigg—down to two in 1969, but since recovered. Coll, with fourteen in 1973, seems relatively secure. On Rum the Conservancy's policy of engaging staff with young families succeeded so well that in 1971 the average age of the whole population was nineteen!

When pupils are few, competition and diverse social contact

are lacking. Twelve-year-olds who have inhabited such small and quiet worlds, who have never played team games, caught a bus or seen a zebra crossing, must find hostel life in traffic-ridden Oban or Fort William strange indeed. Yet they often do well, partly because some good teachers have latterly been attracted by the islands' isolation; but it is not always possible to get Gaelic speakers.

For many years Scottish educational policy has *allowed* Gaelic to be used for giving oral explanations to infants; thereafter English is taught, and all teaching is in English. Seniors may take Gaelic as a special subject. These arrangements, very different from those in Wales and Ireland, have been good for English—which, being learnt, is spoken well—but bad for Gaelic. Marie Kirk, the last Eigg school entrant to speak Gaelic only, enrolled in 1963. In 1973 49 per cent of Tiree's pre-school-age children 'had a knowledge of Gaelic'; but English was the language of the playground on all six islands.

### DOCTORS

The island folk long believed in the magic—later holy—power of water. In the early 1700s water from Fivepennies Well, Eigg, would cure a native of his first disease, but 'if a stranger lie at this well in the night-time it will procure a deformity'. Was the latter notion based on locally developed immunity to contaminated water? As late as 1858 Eigg men refused to drink the water of Dibidil and Papadil, Rum, and insisted on returning to Eigg to quench their thirst.

'Dr Hector' had a practice on Tiree in 1787. Eigg had a 'surgeon' five years later, probably Donald MacAskill (son of the second parish minister) who built Kildonnan House and was drowned within sight of it in 1817. The islands were doctorless in 1836, but a 'medical gentleman' attended Tiree typhus and cholera cases in the 1846 potato famine—perhaps Cornaigbeg's 'An Dotair Mor', traditionally paid in eggs, butter and cheese. Alexander Buchanan served Tiree for fifty-one years from 1860, gave telling evidence to the Napier

Commission and is commemorated by a memorial at Baugh, near the Doctor's House (built in his time and given an excellent new surgery in 1968). He covered Coll until 1881, when a separate doctor arrived for whom a house was built at Arinagour. Until 1897 Small Isles had to send a boat to Arisaig or Tobermory to ask for a doctor. This was quite beyond the means of ordinary folk; from 1855–97 only 12 per cent of Small Isles' deaths were medically certified, compared with 61 per cent on Tiree.

*Diseases*

The islands were vulnerable to imported disease. Measles followed smallpox during the eighteenth century. From 1855 to 1899 tuberculosis, brought by young people working in the south, accounted for 240 deaths on Tiree and 31 on Small Isles, where it was the commonest identified disease. There was also high mortality from respiratory complaints (263 Tiree, 59 Small Isles) due to bad housing, dark winters and lack of fuel—chronically short on Tiree and so scarce on Eigg that by 1863 brushwood had been stripped. Yet Tiree's infant mortality rate was then 71 per 1,000 compared with Scotland's 123, and children under one year old accounted for only 10 per cent of deaths both there and on Small Isles— where childbirth was the most frequent reason for setting out in an open boat in the hope of getting a doctor. Diptheria was common and much feared; the Matheson family who lived at Kilmory, Rum, 5 miles from their nearest neighbours, lost a boy of 7 in 1871 and in September 1873, on successive days, girls of 17 and 8, boys of 12 and 4, and a boy of 6— none had medical attention. Yet the islanders were and are noted for longevity—with a centenarian on Tiree in 1976, and another on Eigg in the 1960s.

*Health services*

From World War I until the advent of the National Health Service, the Highlands and Islands Medical Service guaranteed doctors' incomes, limited fees to those current in urban areas, and helped with accommodation—as in the first doctor's house on Eigg, at the Lodge gates, and the present house at Arinagour, Coll, built by Argyll CC in 1937. ('Grianan', the current Eigg house built in 1955, in NHS days, has never been given a proper surgery.) Two lively women doctors served Small Isles 1928–41. Martha Devon landed a plane on Laig sands in support of the campaign for a Hebridean air ambulance. Josephine Shephard conducted PT classes in the schoolroom, popular both with lasses who took part and lads who watched through the windows.

Since 1968 Tiree has had a fifteen-bed Old People's Home at the former Free Church manse, lovingly run by a Tiresian, Matron Janet Maclean, until her retirement in 1976. With Oban the nearest hospital, a few medical beds would be useful. Small Isles' nearest hospital is at Fort William. The problems of whether, when and how to hospitalise patients have long worried island practitioners. The air ambulance service, which usually flies patients to Glasgow, became available on Tiree when Reef opened before World War II, and to Coll when with C. K. M. Stewart's encouragement the Totronald and Ben Feall emergency strips were laid out in the 1950s. Small Isles lack suitable landing facilities; Fraser Darling's remark, made of Coll when it was served by ferry, may still apply to Eigg, Rum and Muck: 'conditions . . . encountered when taking a sick person . . . for urgent medical treatment are not those which any . . . civilised community should be called upon to endure or which any modern State professing to humane administration should allow to continue'.

Eigg's owner has already shown how a light aeroplane and a seaplane can help, and two casualties of the island's first recorded road accident were taken off by helicopter at Easter 1975; but those excellent arrangements were unofficial. During his twenty-five years as Small Isles' doctor Hector Maclean has twice summoned the lifeboat from Mallaig to carry patients to hospital, and once to take him to an urgent case on Muck. In a 'life or death' situation he can ask for an

RAF helicopter; but 'even today it is desirable that any islander developing a serious illness should do so in reasonable weather'.

The medical future of Tiree seems assured, but a government report of 1967, which took a remarkably optimistic view of the reliability and speed of Hebridean transport, thought that it would be 'sensible' to leave Small Isles (and inferentially Coll) without a doctor.

### Dental treatment

When fish was perforce a prominent item in island diets toothache is said to have been unknown. Thereafter dentistry was much in demand, but until recently it was difficult and expensive to procure. In 1968 John Weatherston, who had previously paid quarterly visits to Tiree, opened that island's first dental surgery; since 1971 he has also covered Coll. On Small Isles the Rum warden's wife is a dental surgeon, and a 'floating dentist' is occasionally seen.

# 14        THE FUTURE

RUM'S community will survive so long as the Nature Conservancy needs the island as an outdoor laboratory, can attract skilled employees with a temporary taste for the extraordinary, and has leaders like Peter Wormell. Extrapolation of the other islands' population-graphs indicates abandonment within a few decades. This will only be avoided if farming can continue to show profit on revenue account, if proprietors continue to forego a 'proper' return on capital, and if living conditions, aided by cash from tourism, can be maintained at an acceptable level.

Island farming is greatly dependent on transport costs, which depend on subsidy, although much might be done by imaginative proposals like the HIDB's scheme for costing sea-transport on a mainland-road basis, and by charging tourists the full cost of their journeys. With a question-mark hovering over Small Isles' livestock boat, there is real cause for concern.

There need be little concern about the willingness of proprietors to forego return on capital, if recent prices are any guide (although taxation policy may alter the picture). In very rounded figures—for such transactions are inevitably complex—Eigg was sold for £50,000 in 1966, £100,000 in 1971 and £250,000 in 1975. The crofters on Eigg, Canna and Tiree are now prospective landowners, for recent government passed legislation allows crofters to buy their land at controlled prices. This measure stems from failure of the Crofters Commission to rescue crofting from nine-teenth-century fragmentation, and from the tenurial rigidity caused by the 1886 Act—and interpretations of it. Tiree crofting needs no rescuing, but is nevertheless affected; and the outcome of a measure enabling crofters to buy, and therefore to sell, perhaps at escalated prices, perhaps to absentees, may or may not benefit the island.

Will people remain willing to live in such remote places? It is pointless to pretend that the islands can ever provide all the rising range of amenities mainland folk now expect. Will increasing appreciation of their assets—beauty, quietness and the island way of life—compensate for missing amenities? Unless the cataclysm of 'oil-related' development overwhelms the islands (a drilling-area has recently been designated west of Tiree) their beauty should remain, given sensible planning control; but confidence was not increased by government's *Coastal Planning Guidelines 1974* which showed only Rum's official coastline as a 'preferred conservation zone'.

Visitors will be an increasing source of supplementary cash and part-time employment; but they need not disturb quietness, for climate and the transport bottleneck should limit numbers. That more subtle asset, the island way of life, is far more fragile. There will always be those who choose to live in such isolated places. Eigg has recently seen two small colonies of monks and most islands now have a leavening of resident incomers from the south—like Barry and Betty Austin whose hard work and sensitive approach have made their Eigg guest-house a real asset to the community.

Yet the full island flavour, which captures the heart, is a product of long continuity. Tiree's community may be large enough to sustain this into the foreseeable future: the Macleans and MacDonalds, the MacFadyens and MacPhails— and the Browns—may long go marching on. Elsewhere the old island families are disappearing, unable to bridge the gap which occurs in every generation when numbers are small and local jobs so few. On Eigg, family continuity is aided by absentee crofters who return each summer, but the Mac-Quarries, the sons of Somerled's son Ruari, have gone after three-quarters of a millennium, and the MacDonalds and MacKinnons have no children in school. The last truly Gaelic people are in danger of disappearing from an island which once saw the investiture of an independent Gaelic potentate, a Lord of the Isles.

This book has not attempted to trace Gaelic culture. The author (to his shame) speaks no Gaelic and has not presumed to deal with something that, by definition, he cannot properly understand. Nevertheless he believes that it is the Gaelic communal way of life which has welded these communities together. Its heyday saw communal Joint Farms; when individual land-holdings were imposed the people transmuted them into communal crofting; even now there is a pervading spirit of unobtrusive neighbourly help—a spirit unwilling, and indeed unable, to submit to modern notions of 'organisation' or 'management'. If island populations are to be kept up—and they must be sustained and increased if amenities are to be maintained—some immigration must take place. Gaelic folk are as kind and friendly as any on earth, but will their way of life mix with that of the incomers, likely to be individualists? Only time will tell.

Meanwhile living memories of the Eigg war dance, of work-songs and fairies, of shinty played on Laig strand on New Year's Day against the haunting beauty of the haunted Coolins of Rum must inevitably shrink into mere tradition, perhaps to be mummified in university theses or trivialised in telly ceilidh. Eigg's last living custom may well be one for the dead; funerals still go sunwise round old St Donnan's chapel, tracing a path more ancient than Christianity. Yet something may remain. Dances are still 'made' in the public hall. There is Gaelic fire in the snap of Duncan Ferguson's fiddle. Donald MacKinnon's and Angus Kirk's accordions may not be strictly Gaelic, but they set the feet tapping all the same. And when the swelling skirl of the Doctor's bagpipes sets the room afire for the eightsome reel, and islanders, incomers and visitors alike spin and sway to the dance, who can think that an auld song is nearing its end?

# SINGING SAND

There are singing sands at Morar, Lochaline, on the Northumberland coast, Cardigan Bay, Studland Bay, in the Channel Isles and doubtless elsewhere. In 1891 it was found that singing sand had rounded dust-free grains mostly within a narrow size-range, and that it would not sing after repeated pounding but regained full voice after being washed. In 1937 a Japanese report on local sands and on a sample from Camas Sgiotaig associated singing with a high coefficient of friction. After the war Japanese Radio broadcast sounds of various sands including some from Eigg; it was thought that singing occurred when sudden compression expelled air from between the grains. In the 1960s a Newcastle University group concluded that grains need not be rounded

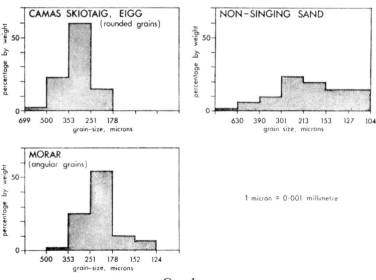

Graph 7
Singing sand, grain-size in microns

(Morar sands are angular), that sound varied with grain-size, that its volume varied with viscosity of the ambient media (being greater in water than air) and that the degree of restraint was important (below some critical degree there was no sound; increased restraint resulted in sounds of higher frequency). All investigators have agreed that most grains must be of similar size.

The following hypothesis is based on Newcastle data. Imagine all grains to be small equal-sized balls disposed in close-fitting layers. The sole of a walker's shoe induces pressure and forward movement in the topmost layer. Each ball contacted rolls forward, firstly by climbing up the balls on which it rests, then by falling down them. Similar 'up-and-down-and-forward' motions are simultaneously transmitted to balls in lower layers. Most balls move similarly and simultaneously, and the consequent sounds therefore aggregate—hence 'singing'.

Should restraint be lessened grains would become less closely packed—there would be minute gaps between them. The 'up-and-down' components of motion would be reduced and a different note would therefore result. Should restraint be further reduced, to the point at which packing ceased to be orderly, motions would be neither similar nor simultaneous and the sounds would not aggregate.

Finally, the ambient medium must influence the speed of movement induced in the grains by any given force applied, and therefore the quality of sound emitted.

# DEAN MONRO'S ACCOUNT, 1549

### EGGE

. . . gude mayne land, with ane paroch kirk in it, with mony solenne geis; very gude for store, namelie for scheip, with ane heavin for hieland Galayis.

### RUM

. . . ane forrest full of heich montanes and abundante of little deiris in it, quhilk deiris will never be slane downwith but the principall settis man be in the heich of the hills, because the deir will be callit upwart ay be tynchellis, or without tynchellis they will up a forte. In this Ile thair will be gottin about Beltane als mony fowl nestis full of eggis about the mure as men pleases to gadder, and that becaus the fowls hes few to start thame except deiris. This Ile stands fra the west to the eist in lenth, and perteins to the Laird of Coll callit Mcane abrie. Mony solenne geis are in this Ile. This land obeyis to Mcgillane of Doward instantlie.

### CANNAY

. . . fair mane land, four mile lang inhabite and manurit, with an paroch kirk in it, gude for corn, girsing and fisching, with an falcon nest in it. It perteins to the Abbot of Colmkill.

### ELLAN NA MUK

. . . ane verie fertile frutfull Ile of cornis and girsing for all store, verie gude for fische, inhabite and manurit, with ane gude falcon nest, perteining to the Bischop of the Iles, with ane gude hieland heavin in it, the entrie at the west cheek of it.

*Ellan na Neach*
. . . gude for horse and uther store, perteining to the Bischop of the Iles.

# APPENDIX B

. . . Ane mane fertile Ile inhabite and manurit, with ane castell and ane paroch kirk in it, gude for fishing and fowlers, with ane utter fine Falcons nest in it.

*Gunna*
. . . manurit and inhabite, gude for corn, store and fishing.

. . . ane mane laich fertile fruitful cuntrie . . . All inhabite and manurit with twa paroche kirkis in it, ane fresh water loch, with ane auld castell\*. Na cuntrie may be mair fertile of corn, and very gude for wild fowls and for fische, with ane gude heavin for heiland galayis.

\*On an island in Loch an Eilean, approached by drawbridge: presumably the Duarts' Tiree headquarters. The keep walls were incorporated in the current Island House, built 1748, for the 3rd Duke's factor; causeway made somewhat later (traditionally by forced labour). Front gables probably 1874. Occupied by factors into Major MacLennan's time.

# SHIPPING ROUTES AND STEAMERS

The information given is necessarily incomplete and approximate

### SMALL ISLES

| route | years | steamer | built | GRT |
|-------|-------|---------|-------|-----|
| lasgow–Oban–EIGG–Arisaig– | 1857–69 | PS *Clansman I* | 1855 | 414 |
| kye–Lewis | 1862–5 | SS *Clydesdale I* | 1862 | 403 |
| rom 1930 cargo only; RUM | 1870–1909 | SS *Clansman II* | 1870 | 600 |
| nd CANNA to 1949, EIGG to | 1881–1930 | SS *Claymore I* | 1881 | 726 |
| 952 | 1930–52 | SS *Clydesdale II* | 1905 | 401 |
| ban– | 1881–98 | SS *Hebridean* (M) | 1881 | 314 |
| IGG (not summer until 1914)– | 1881–1903 | SS *Staffa III* | 1861 | 197 |
| risaig*–RUM–CANNA–Skye– | 1891–1904 | SS *Flowerdale* | 1878 | 485 |
| uter Isles | 1903–08 | SS *Lapwing II* | 1903 | 211 |
| ircular, both directions | 1904–21 | SS *Plover III* | 1904 | 191 |
| eased 1921 | 1909–17 | SS *Lochiel II* | 1908 | 241 |
| ban–EIGG–Arisaig*– | 1863–81 | PS *Pioneer I* | 1844 | 144 |
| yle–Gairloch | 1877–85 | PS *Glencoe II* | 1846 | 193 |
| immer only. Ceased 1914 | 1885–92 | PS *Grenadier* | 1885 | 321 |
| | 1892–1914 | PS *Gael* | 1867 | 419 |
| allaig–EIGG–RUM–CANNA– | 1921–30 | SS *Plover III* | 1904 | 191 |
| uter Isles–Kyle–Mallaig | 1921–30 | SS *Cygnet II* | 1904 | 191 |
| ircular, both directions | 1930–64 | MV *Lochmor* | 1930 | 452 |
| [allaig–EIGG–RUM–CANNA | 1964 | MV *Loch Arkaig* | 1942 | 179 |
| Mallaig | | | | |
| AUCK from 1966 except Dec– | 1965–75 | MV *Western Isles* (W) | 1940s | 52 |
| eb) Mon Wed Thu; Sat (2 runs | | | | |
| summer) | | | | |
| ircular, both directions | | | | |

*Arisaig (Rhu Pier) to 1901; Mallaig thereafter

# *APPENDIX C*

COLL AND TIREE

| *route* | *years* | *steamer* | *built* | GRT |
|---|---|---|---|---|
| Glasgow–Oban–Mull–COLL– | 1862–8 | SS *Islesman* (O) | 1858 | 14[illegible] |
| TIREE–Outer Isles | 1868–75 | SS *Dunvegan Castle* (O) | 1868 | 29[illegible] |
| Smaller vessels via Crinan | 1874–80 | SS *Lady Ambrosine* (M) | 1874 | 11[illegible] |
| Canal | 1875–1948 | SS *Dunara Castle* (O) | 1875 | 42[illegible] |
| | 1878–97 | SS *Aros Castle* (O) | 1878 | 14[illegible] |
| | 1890–7 | SS *Quirang* (M) | 1870 | 46[illegible] |
| | 1898–1942 | SS *Hebrides I* (M) | 1898 | 58[illegible] |
| | 1942–46 | SS *Lochgorm II* | 1866 | 63[illegible] |
| cargo only | 1946–52 | SS *Hebrides I* (MO) | 1898 | 58[illegible] |
| | 1952–76 | MV *Loch Carron* | 1950 | 65[illegible] |
| Oban–COLL–TIREE– | 1881–1903 | SS *Staffa III* | 1861 | 19[illegible] |
| Bunessan, Mull | 1881–1908 | SS *Fingal II* | 1877 | 12[illegible] |
| | 1908–09 | SS *Lochiel II* | 1908 | 14[illegible] |
| | 1909–14 | SS *Dirk* | 1909 | 18[illegible] |
| Oban–COLL–TIREE–Outer | 1914–21 | SS *Plover III* | 1904 | 19[illegible] |
| Isles | 1921–30 | SS *Cygnet II* | 1904 | 19[illegible] |
| Some services also called RUM, | | | | |
| CANNA | | | | |
| Oban–COLL–TIREE–Barra– | 1930–55 | MV *Lochearn* | 1930 | 45[illegible] |
| South Uist. Out: Mon Wed Fri | 1942–6 | SS *Hebrides I*† | 1898 | 58[illegible] |
| Back: Tue Thu Sat | 1955–74 | MV *Claymore II* | 1955 | 102[illegible] |
| From 1973 to COLL and TIREE | 1972–3 | MV *Loch Seaforth* | 1947 | 112[illegible] |
| only, in summer, 3 or 4 times a | 1974–5 | CF *Iona* (50 cars) | 1970 | 119[illegible] |
| week | 1975 | CF *Columba II* (50 cars) | 1964 | 210[illegible] |

†RAF service, to Tiree only.

All vessels Hutcheson/MacBrayne except: M = McCallum; O = Orme; W = Bruce Watt, Mallaig; SS = steamship; PS = paddle steamer; MV = motor vessel; CF = car ferry.

# BIBLIOGRAPHY

Sources are listed under chapters; in many cases those quoted have also been used in subsequent sections of the book.

*Chapter 2*

CAMPBELL, J. L. 'A home on Canna', *Scots Mag* (Feb 1953)
——.'Farming in the Hebrides', *Scottish Farmer* (Jan 1942)
CAMPBELL, W. A. et al. *Musical Sand* (Proc Univ Newcastle Phil Soc 1961–8)
CHAPMAN, R. W. *Johnson's Journey to the Western Isles of Scotland* (and Boswell's *Journal*) (1970)
COULL, J. R. 'The Island of Tiree', *Scot Geog Mag* (April 1962)
CREGEEN, E. R. (ed) *Argyll Estate Instructions 1771–1805* (Scot Hist Soc, Edinburgh 1964)
DARLING, F. F. et al. *West Highland Survey* (1955)
DONALDSON, MARGARET E. M. *Wanderings in the Western Highlands and Islands* (nd c1921)
HARKER, A. *The Geology of the Small Isles of Inverness-shire* (Glasgow 1908)
——. (posth). *The West Highlands and the Hebrides* (1941)
MacDOUGAL, H. and REV H. CAMERON. *Handbook to the islands of Coll and Tiree* (Glasgow nd c1937)
MacECHERN, REV D. *Place Names of Coll* (Trans Gael Soc Inverness, vol XXIX, 1914–19)
MacEWEN, L. *A Guide to Eigg and Muck* (Privately published 1973)
MILLER, H. (posth). *The Cruise of the Betsey* (Edinburgh 1858)
POTTLE, F. A. et al. *Boswell's Journal of a tour to the Hebrides 1773* (1963)
RICHEY, J. E. et al. *The Geology of Ardnamurchan, north-west Mull and Coll* (Edinburgh 1930)
ROBERTSON, REV C. M. *Topography and traditions of Eigg* (Proc Gael Soc Inverness, 24 Feb 1898)

M                                                                 193

# BIBLIOGRAPHY

SINCLAIR, SIR J. (ed) *Statistical Account of Scotland* (Edinburgh 1791–8)

WAUGH, E. *The Limping Pilgrim* (Manchester 1883)

British Regional Geology. *Scotland, the tertiary volcanic districts* 3rd ed (HMSO 1961)

*Chapter 3*

CAMPBELL, G. D. (8th Duke of Argyll). *Autobiography and Memoirs* (ed Dowager Duchess) (Edinburgh 1906)

DARLING, F. F. and BOYD, J. M. *The Highlands and Islands* (New Naturalist series, 2nd ed, 1969)

MACNEICE, L. *I Crossed the Minch* (1938)

TINN, A. B. *This Weather of Ours* (1946)

Meteorological Office (HMSO)

    *Climatological memo* 56

    *Climatological atlas of the British Isles* (MO 488) (1952)

    SHELLARD, H. C. *Tables of surface wind speed and direction over the United Kingdom* (MO 792) (1968)

    *Average annual rainfall 1916–50*

    *Weather in Home Waters* Vol III *The Western Approaches to Great Britain and Ireland* (1940)

Admiralty Sailing Directions—*The West Coast Pilot*

Sailing Directions and Anchorages—*West coast of Scotland* (Clyde Crusing Club, Glasgow 1966)

*Chapter 4*

Anon (Sheriff Nicholson). *Lay of the Beanmhor* (privately published Edinburgh 1867)

Anon (probably Calder Ross). 'St Donnan the Great' *Scottish Notes and Queries* (Nov–Dec 1935)

BALFOUR, LADY F. *Lady Victoria Campbell, a memoir* (nd c1912)

BEVERIDGE, E. *Coll and Tiree, their prehistoric forts and ecclesiastical antiquities* (Edinburgh 1903)

CAMERON, REV A. *Reliquiae Celticae* (Inverness 1894)

CAMPBELL, N. D. (ed). 'An old Tiree rental for the year 1662', *Scottish Notes and Queries*

DUNCAN, A. A. M. and BROWN, A. L. *Argyll and the Islands in the early Middle Ages* (Proc Soc Ant Scot 1956–7)

GIBLIN, C. (ed). *The Irish Franciscan mission to Scotland 1619–46* (Dublin 1964)

GORDON, SETON. *Highways and byways in the West Highlands* (1949)

GRANT, ISOBEL F. *The Macleods* (1959)

GREGORY, D. *History of the West Highlands and Islands* (Edinburgh 1836; 2nd ed London 1881)

KERMACK, W. R. *The Scottish Highlands* (Edinburgh 1957)

LOCKHART, J. G. *Life of Sir Walter Scott* (Lib Standard Biogs 1904)

MACDONALD, A. and A. *Clan Donald* (Inverness 1896)

MACKIE, E. W. 'Brochs and the Hebridean Iron Age', *Antiquity* vol 34 (1965)

——. 'Radiocarbon dates and the Scottish Iron Age', *Antiquity* vol 43

MACLEAN, J. P. *History of the Clan Maclean* (Cincinnati 1889)

MACPHAIL, J. R. N. (ed). *Highland Papers* vol 1–4 (Scot Hist Soc 1914–34)

MACPHERSON, N. *Notes on the antiquities of the island of Eigg* (Proc Soc Ant Scot 11 Mar 1878)

MACTAVISH, D. C. (ed). *Minutes of the Synod of Argyll 1639–61* (Scot Hist Soc 1943–4)

MARTIN, MARTIN. *A Description of the Western Isles of Scotland* (1703; new ed Stirling 1934)

MILLAR, A. H. (ed). *A selection of the Forfeited Estates Papers* (Scot Hist Soc 1909)

MITCHELL, SIR A. (ed). *MacFarlane's Geographical Collections* (Scot Hist Soc 1906–8)

MUNRO, DEAN DONALD. *A Description of the Western Isles of Scotland called Hybrides* (c1549; new ed Stirling 1934)

REEVES, REV W. *The Island of Tiree* (Ulster Jour Arch Belfast 1854)

ROSS, D. *Contents of shell-heaps found on the Island of Coll* (Proc Soc Ant Scot 14 Feb 1881)

SINCLAIR, REV A. MACLEAN. *Clan Gillean* (Charlotte Town 1899)

SKENE, W. F. *Celtic Scotland* (Edinburgh 1877)

WILSON, J. *A voyage round the coasts of Scotland and the Isles* (Edinburgh 1842)

4th and 6th Reports of the Historical Manuscripts Commission (1877)

Catalogue of the National Museum of Antiquities (Edinburgh 1892)

9th Report of the Royal Commission on Ancient and Historical Monuments (Scotland). *The Outer Hebrides, Skye and the Small Isles* (1928)

# BIBLIOGRAPHY

Chapter 5

BELL, R. F. (ed). *Memorials of John Murray of Broughton 1740–1747* (Scot Hist Soc 1898)

CREGEEN, E. R. 'The Tacksmen and their successors', *Scottish Studies* 13. (School of Scottish Studies, Univ of Edin nd)

DONALDSON, MARGARET E. M. *Further wanderings, mostly in Argyll* (nd c1927)

FERGUSON, SIR J. *Argyll in the '45* (1951)

FORBES, REV R. *The Lyon in Mourning* (Scot Hist Soc 1895–6)

GIBSON, J. S. *Ships of the '45* (1967)

MACKERRALL, A. *The Clan Campbell* (Edinburgh 1957)

PATON, REV H. *The Clan Campbell* (abstracts of entries in the Sheriff Court Books of Argyll) (Edinburgh 1913)

PREBBLE, J. *Glencoe* (1966)

*Miscellanea Scotica*: A collection of Tracts. (Glasgow 1820)


Chapter 6

AYLING, S. E. *The Georgian century 1714–1837* (1966)

DUNLOP, JEAN. *The British Fisheries Society 1786–1893*: thesis for PhD (Univ of Edin 1952)

FERGUSON, SIR J. 'The Fishery Society and its foundations', *Scots Mag* (April 1934)

GASKELL, P. *Morvern transformed* (1968)

JAMESON, R. *Mineralogy of the Scottish Isles* (Edinburgh 1800)

LEYDEN, J. *Journal of a tour in the Highlands and Western Isles of Scotland in 1800* (Edinburgh 1900)

McCULLOCH, J. *The Highlands and Western Islands of Scotland* (1824)

MACDONALD, J. *A general view of agriculture in the Hebrides* (1811)

MACKAY, I. *Clanranald's tacksmen of the late 18th century* (Trans Gael Soc Inverness XLIV 1964)

OTTER, W. *Life and remains of Edward Daniel Clarke DD* (1834)

PENNANT, T. *A tour in Scotland and voyage to the Hebrides 1772* (per Pinkerton, J. General collection of travels vol 3 1809)

DE SAUSSURE, L. A. N. *Voyage en Ecosse at aux Isles Hebride* (Geneva 1821)

SMOUT, T. C. *A history of the Scottish people 1560–1830* 2nd ed (1970)

WALKER, J. *An economical history of the Hebrides and Islands of Scotland* (Edinburgh 1808)

Report from the Select Committee on Emigration from the United Kingdom (1827)

4th Report by the Commissioners on Religious Instruction, Scotland (1838)

Report of the Select Committee on Emigration (Scotland) (1841)

*The New Statistical Account of Scotland* (Edinburgh 1845)

Report (by Sir J. M'Neill) to the Board of the Supervision on the Western Highlands and Islands (1851)

Report of HM Commissioners of Inquiry into the conditions of crofters and cottars in the Highlands and Islands of Scotland (1884)

List of buildings of Architectural or Historic interest (Scottish Development Department)


*Chapter 7*

FERGUSON, SIR J. 'An East Indiaman on Canna', *Scots Mag* (Nov 1934)

MacDONALD, D. A. (ed). *Hugh MacKinnon.* Tocher 10 (School of Scottish Studies 1973)

MacDONALD, J. W. *A Vacation in the Scottish Highlands* (Los Angeles 1930)

MacDOUGALL, J. L. *History of Inverness County Nova Scotia* (privately printed in Canada nd; c1928)

Correspondence relating to the Measures Adopted for Relief of the Distress in Scotland (Parliamentary Accounts and Papers 1847)


*Chapter 8*

BALFOUR, LADY F. *Ne Obliviscaris* (nd c1935)

CAMERON, J. *The old and the new Highlands and Hebrides* (1912)

CAMPBELL, J. D. S. (9th Duke of Argyll). *Passages from the past* (1907)

CUMMING, MISS C. F. GORDON. *In the Hebrides* New ed (1883)

FINLAY, C. K. 'Island of prosperous crofters', *Scots Mag* (June 1965)

FREER, MISS A. GOODRICH. *Outer Isles* (1902)

MACKENZIE, H. R. and FRASER-MACKINTOSH, C. *Yachting and electioneering in the Hebrides* (privately published nd; c1886)

MACLEAN, N. *Set free* (1949)

M'NAUGHTON, T. 'The crofter risings in Tiree', *People's Journal* (14 Nov 1925)

*Summer tours in Scotland*: David MacBrayne Ltd (1906)

# BIBLIOGRAPHY

Crofters Holdings (Scotland) Act (1886)
Report of the Royal Commission (Highlands and Islands) (1892)
Report of the Select Committee on the Western Highlands and
  Islands of Scotland (1928)
(Press) reports of the local proceedings of the Economic Com-
  mittee of the Scottish Development Council (1937)

*Chapter 9*

BULLOUGH, J. (posth) *Speeches and letters*, ed Alexandra Bullough
  (privately published 1892)
CROSSLEY, R. S. 'Accrington Captains of industry, *Accrington
  Observer and Times* (1930)
DUNNET, A. M. *It's Too Late in the Year* (Bath 1969)
ENGELBRACHT, H. C. and HANIGHEN, F. C. *Merchants of death*
  (1934)
GRANT, SIR F. J. *The Faculty of Advocates in Scotland* (Edinburgh
  1944)
HAGGARD, H. RIDER. *A farmer's year* (1906)
MACKENZIE, COMPTON. *My Life and Times: Octave 7 1931–38*
  (1968)
WALKER, W. *Reminiscences, academic, ecclesiastic and scholastic*
  (1904)
'WBB'. 'Brigadier-General E. M. P. Stewart of Coll', *Royal
  Engineers Jour* (Dec 1942)
WEIR, T. 'Campbell of Canna', *Scots Mag* (July 1971)
*Quasi Cursores*. Aberdeen University—Tercentenary portraits.
  (Aberdeen 1884)

*Chapter 10*

BLATCHFORD, J. G. 'Breeding Birds of Coll', *Jour Scot Ornith-
  ologists Club* vol 6 no 5 (1971)
BOYD, J. M. 'The Birds of Tiree and Coll', *British Birds* (Feb–
  Mar 1958)
CONNELL, C. G. 'Bird Notes from Eigg', *Scot Naturalist* (Sep–Oct
  1926)
DUNCAN, URSULA K. *Isles of Coll and Tiree* (Proc Botanical Soc
  Brit Isles vol 7, 1967–9)
EVANS, P. R. and FLOWER, W. U. 'The birds of the Small Isles',
  *Jour Scot Ornithologists Club* vol 4 no 6 (1967)
GILLAIN, BEATRICE, and JACOBS, G. R. 'Breeding Birds of Tiree',
  *Jour Scot Ornithologists Club* vol 6 no 5 (1971)
GRAY, R. *Birds of the west of Scotland* (1871)

HARRISON, J. W. H. 'Fauna and flora of the Inner and Outer Hebrides', *Nature* (17 June 1939)

------. 'Flora and fauna of the Inner and Outer Hebrides', *Nature* (1 Feb 1951)

------. (et al). *The Flora of the Isles of Coll Tiree and Gunna* (Proc Univ Durham Phil Soc vol X part 4 Dec 1941)

RAVEN, J. E. 'Alien plant introductions on the Isle of Rhum', *Nature* (15 Jan 1949)

SMITH, A. D. B. ' "Wild" goats in Scotland', *British Goat Society's Yearbook* (1932)

WHITEHEAD, G. K. *The Wild Goats of Great Britain and Ireland* (Newton Abbot 1972)

Isle of Rhum National Nature Reserve, Kinloch Glen and South Side nature trails. NERC for Nature Conservancy (Edinburgh nd c1970)

*The Natural History of Canna and Sanday* (Proc Royal Physical Soc pt 1 vol xxiii, Edinburgh 1939)

*Chapter 11*

CAMPBELL, J. L. *Statements on behalf of the Island of Canna* (privately published 1964)

DUCKWORTH, C. L. D. and LANGMUIR, G. E. *Clyde River and other steamers* 3rd ed (1972)

------. *West Highland steamers* 3rd ed (1967)

ELLESMERE, EARL OF. 'The Skerryvore Lighthouse', *Quarterly Review* (1858)

FRESSON, CAPT E. E. *Air Road to the Isles* (1963)

HALDANE, A. R. B. *New ways through the Glens* (1962)

------. *Three centuries of Scottish posts* (Edinburgh 1971)

KENNEDY-FRASER, MARJORIE and MACLEOD, REV K. *Songs of the Hebrides* (1909; new ed 1922)

MACDONALD, C. M. (ed) *Third Statistical Account of Scotland— Argyll* (1961)

McINTYRE, GRP CAPT D. F. 'Development of air transport in Scotland', *Scot Geog Mag* (Sep 1945)

McKEAN, R. *Lifeline to the Islands* (Scot Public Services 1963)

MEEK, D. E. 'Puffers', *Scots Mag* (April 1969)

PENNELL, J. and E. R. *Our journey to the Hebrides* (1890)

REA, F. G. *A school in South Uist* (ed J. L. Campbell) (1964)

ROBERTSON, R. G. 'By sea to the Western Isles', *Ships Monthly* (Feb–Oct 1969)

SMITH, JANET A. *RLS—collected poems* 2nd ed (1971)

# BIBLIOGRAPHY

STEVENSON, A. *An account of the Skerryvore lighthouse* (Edinburgh 1848)

TAYLOR, I. C. *Highland communications: An Comunn Gaidhealach* (1969)

THOMAS, J. *The West Highland Railway* (Newton Abbot 1965)

Reports of the Board of Agriculture for Scotland 1913–27

Report of the Rural Transport (Scotland) Committee (1919)

*Summer Tours in Scotland*: David MacBrayne (1884)

MacBrayne's Contracts 1921, 1928

*One hundred years of progress*: David MacBrayne Ltd (1951)

*Visit the romantic Western Isles and lone St Kilda* (nd c1929)

*Aviation in Scotland* (R. Aeronautical Soc, Glasgow 1966)

## Chapter 12

MARTIN, C. 'Diving around Coll', *Scots Mag* (May 1970)

SHEDDEN, H. *The Story of Lorn, its Isles and Oban* (Oban 1938)

SIMPSON, W. D. *Breachacha Castle in the Isle of Coll* (Trans Glasgow Arch Soc vol x 1941)

TURNER, D. J. and DUNBAR, J. G. *Breachacha Castle, Coll*: Excavation and Field Survey 1965–8 (Proc Soc Ant Scot)

Reports of the Crofters Commission

Reports of the Highlands and Islands Development Board

Reports of the Nature Conservancy

Reports of the Hill Farming Research Organisation

## Chapter 13

BELLESHEIM, CANON A. (Trans D. O. Hunter-Blair). *History of the Catholic Church of Scotland* (1888)

BLUNDELL, DOM O. *The Catholic Highlands of Scotland* (Edinburgh 1917)

CAMPBELL, J. L. *Gaelic in Scottish Education and Life* (Edinburgh 1950)

——. 'The Catholic Church in the Hebrides 1560–1760', *The Tablet* (31 Dec 1955)

——. and THOMSON D. *Edward Lhuyd in the Scottish Highlands 1699–1700* (Oxford 1963)

EWING, REV W. (ed) *Annals of the Free Church of Scotland* (Edinburgh 1914)

FERGUSON, T. 'A note on mortality in the Islands of Barra and Tiree during the second half of the nineteenth century', *Scot Med Jour* 7 (1962)

INNES, C. (ed) *Origines Parochiales Scotiae* (Edinburgh 1851–5)

MACDONALD, REV R. 'Bishop Scott in the West Highlands', *Innes Review* (Autumn 1966)

NICOLSON, A. *Report on the state of education in the Hebrides* (Edinburgh 1866)

SCOTT, H. (ed) *Fasti Ecclesiae Scoticanae* new ed (Edinburgh 1915–28)

SWANSON, REV J. *A leisure hour in the floating Manse* (Edinburgh 1844)

*Moral statistics of the Highlands and Islands of Scotland.* Inverness Soc for Education of the Poor in the Highlands (Inverness 1826)

*Disruption Worthies of the Highlands* (Edinburgh 1877)

*Baptist Handbook* 1971

*Catholic Directory* 1970

Fasti of the United Free Church 1956

Report of the Committee on General Medical Services in the Highlands and Islands (1967)


GENERAL

*The Times, Oban Times, Glasgow Herald, Hansard*


*Other written sources*

Clanranald Papers

Department of Agriculture for Scotland, Returns and Papers

Diaries of Michael Packenham Edgeworth (Eigg 1857–81) and of Olive Butler (Eigg 1913 and 1950); MacPherson family letters and papers (through the kindness of Michael Butler)

Kirk Session Records, Small Isles Coll and Tiree

Ordnance Survey Name Books

Parish Council Minute Book, Small Isles

Registers of Births Marriages and Deaths, Small Isles

School Board Minute Book, Eigg

School Logs Acha, Coll; Cornaigmore, Tiree; Eigg, Muck and Rum

Scottish Office Papers

# ACKNOWLEDGEMENTS

M Y gratitude goes to the innumerable people, organisations and authorities who have been so generous and especially to:

*Proprietors, their descendants or representatives*
The Viscount of Arbuthnott; William Brown; Michael Butler; Robert Evans; Bernard Farnham-Smith; Lady Francis Ferguson; Elizabeth Gibb; Lawrence MacEwen; Ian Mackenzie; Major Iain MacLennan; Nature Conservancy; the Hon Sir Steven Runciman; Keith Schellenberg and R. V. G. Thom.

*Libraries and newspapers*
Aberdeen University Library; *Accrington Observer and Times*; Accrington Public Library; Birmingham Reference Library; General Register House, Edinburgh; National Library of Scotland; Nova Scotia Public Records Office; St Andrew's University Library; *Scots Magazine*; Scottish Central Library; West Highland Museum Library, and Westminster City Library.

*Scholars and experts*
Eric Cregeen, Seton Gordon, Frank Green, A. R. B. Haldane, Michael Laird, Graham Langmuir, T. Mackenzie (Acha school log, Coll) Ewen MacKie, Mrs C. W. Murray, J. Drew Smith (thesis on Rum) and Denis Turner.

*Island people*
RUM    Ian Cameron, George MacNaughton, Winifred Polson, Peter Wormell.

# ACKNOWLEDGEMENTS

CANNA   Jessie MacKinnon.

MUCK   Ann Cunningham, Charles MacDonald, Elizabeth MacEwen.

COLL   Major Nicholas Maclean Bristol, Betty MacDougal, Alastair Oliphant.

TIREE   Robert Beck, the late A. G. H. Bruton, Ian Christie, W. Groat, Lachlan MacFadyen, Janet Maclean, the late Malcolm Maclean, Mona Maclean, R. M. MacPherson, Robert Petrie.

EIGG   Duncan Ferguson, Fergus Gowans, Margaret and the late Donald Kirk, Lachlan MacDonald, Dr Hector Maclean, Dugald MacKinnon, Peggy and Angus MacKinnon, Mary Snowman, Peter Stanley (ornithologist and honorary *Fachach*)—indeed to all my friends the island people.

Finally to the late Hugh Mackinnon of Cleadale, Eigg, who caused this book to be started; to Donald Meek of Caoles, Tiree, whose generous help enabled it to be extended to cover Coll and Tiree on the death of John Barr, the publishers' original author for those islands; to John Lorne Campbell of Canna for kindnesses, suggestions and corrections throughout its progress; and to my wife for typing and retyping, patience and encouragement, without which it could never have been completed.

Wolverton, Stratford-on-Avon
Kildonnan Brae Cottage, Isle of Eigg
1970–6

# INDEX

# INDEX